AFTER-DINNER AND OTHER
SPEECHES

AFTER-DINNER AND OTHER SPEECHES

BY

JOHN D. LONG

Essay Index Reprint Series

BOOKS FOR LIBRARIES PRESS
FREEPORT, NEW YORK

First Published 1895
Reprinted 1972

Library of Congress Cataloging in Publication Data

Long, John Davis, 1838-1915.
   After-dinner and other speeches.

   (Essay index reprint series)
   Reprint of the 1895 ed.
   I. Title.
PS2249.L85A69 1972   815'.4   72-4550
ISBN 0-8369-2958-6

These speeches, made when I was in public life, may have some value as a partial reflection of the public sentiment, and of the topics and occasions, of a generation in Massachusetts, which is now more past than present, and to which, mindful of the kindnesses and opportunities it gave me, I gratefully inscribe them.

Hingham, February 22, 1895.

CONTENTS.

CONTENTS.

DANIEL WEBSTER.

THE HUNDREDTH ANNIVERSARY OF HIS BIRTH, MARSHFIELD CLUB,
PARKER HOUSE, BOSTON, JANUARY 18, 1882.

IT is but a poor tribute that even the most eloquent
voice, least of all mine, can pay for Massachusetts to the
memory of her mightiest man of state and her greatest
orator. Among her sons he towers like the massive shaft
on Bunker Hill, upon the base and crest of which his name
is emblazoned clearer than if chiseled deep in its granite
cubes. For years he was her synonym. Among the
states he sustained her at that proud height which Winthrop and Sam Adams gave her in the colonial and provincial days. With what matchless grandeur he defended
her! With what overwhelming power he impressed her
convictions upon the national life! God seems to appoint
men to special work; and, that done, the very effort of
its achievement exhausts them, and they rise not again to
the summit of their meridian. So it was with Webster.
He knows little of written constitutions and frames of
government who does not know that they exist less in
the letter than in the interpretation and construction of
the letter. In this light it is not too much to say that the
constitution of the United States, as it existed when it
sustained our country through the recent and greatest
peril that ever tested it, and as it reflected the popular
sense, was the crystallization of the mind of Webster.
It came from its framers, and was accepted by some of
our own, in New England, as a compact of states, sove-

reign in all but certain enumerated powers delegated to a central government. He made it the crucible of a welded union, the charter of one great country, the United States of America. He made those states' a nation and enfolded them in its single banner. It was the overwhelming logic of his discussion, the household familiarity of his simple but irresistible statement, that gave us munition with which to fight the war for the preservation of the union and the abolition of slavery. It was his eloquence, clear as crystal and precipitating itself in the schoolbooks and literature of a people, which had trained up the generation of twenty-five years ago to regard this nation as one, to love its flag with a patriotism that knew no faction or section, to be loyal to the whole country, and to find in its constitution power to suppress any hand or combination raised against it. The great rebellion of 1861 went down hardly more before the cannon of Grant and Farragut than the thunder of Webster's reply to Hayne. He knew not the extent of his own achievement. His greatest failure was that he rose not to the height and actual stroke of his own resistless argument, and that he lacked the sublimed inspiration, the disentanglement and the courage to let the giant he had created go upon his errand, first of force and then through that of surer peace. He had put the work and genius of more than an ordinary lifetime of service into the arching and knitting of the union, and this he could not bear to put to the final test. His great heart was sincere in the prayer that his eyes might not behold the earthquake that would shake it to those foundations, which, though he knew it not, he had made so strong that a succeeding generation saw them stand the shock as the oak withstands the storm. Men are not gods, and it needed in him that he should rise to a moral sublimity and daring as lofty as the intellectual heights above which he soared with unequaled strength. So had he been godlike.

A great man touches the heart of the people as well as their intelligence. They not only admire, they also love him. It sometimes seems as if they sought in him some weakness of our common human nature, that they might chide him for it, then forgive it, and so endear him to themselves the more. Massachusetts had her friction with the younger Adams only to lay him away with profounder honor, and to remember him devotedly as the defender of the right of petition and "the old man eloquent." She forgave the overweening conceit of Sumner; she revoked her unjust censure of him, and now points her youth to him in his high niche as the unsullied patriot without fear and without reproach, who stood and spoke for equal rights, and whose last great service was to demand and enforce his country's just claims against the dishonorable trespass of the cruisers of that England he had so much admired. Massachusetts smote and broke the heart of Webster, her idol, and then broke her own above his grave, and to-day writes his name highest upon her roll of statesmen. It seems disjointed to say that, with such might as his, the impression that comes from his face upon the wall, as from his silhouette upon the background of our history, is that of sadness, — the sadness of the great deep eyes, the sadness of the lonely shore he loved, and by which he sleeps. But the story of Webster from the beginning is the very pathos of romance. A minor chord runs through it like the tenderest note in a song. What eloquence of tears is in that narrative, which reveals in this giant of intellectual strength the heart, the single, loving heart of a child, and in which he describes the winter sleigh-ride up the New Hampshire hills, when his father told him that, at whatever cost, he should have a college education, and he, too full to speak, laid his head upon his father's shoulder and wept!

The greatness of Webster and his title to enduring gratitude have two illustrations. He taught the people of the United States, in the simplicity of common understanding, the principles of the constitution and government of the country; and he wrought for them, in a style of matchless strength and beauty, the literature of statesmanship. From his lips flowed the discussion of constitutional law, of economic philosophy, of finance, of international right, of national grandeur, and of the whole range of high public themes, so clear and judicial that it was no longer discussion, but judgment. To-day, and so it will be while the republic endures, the student and the legislator turn to the full fountain of his statement for the enunciation of these principles. What other authority is quoted, or holds even the second or third place? Even his words have imbedded themselves in the common phraseology, and come to the tongue like passages from the psalms or the poets. I do not know that a sentence or a word of Sumner's repeats itself in our every-day parlance. The exquisite periods of Everett are recalled like the consummate work of some master of music, but no note or refrain sings itself over and over again to our ears. The brilliant eloquence of Choate is like the flash of a bursting rocket, lingering upon the retina indeed after it has faded from the wings of night, but as illusive of our grasp as spray-drops that glisten in the sun. The fiery enthusiasm of Andrew did, indeed, burn some of his heart-beats forever into the sentiment of Massachusetts; but Webster made his language the very household words of a nation. They are the library of a people. They inspired and still inspire patriotism. They taught and still teach loyalty. They are the schoolbook of the citizen. They are the inwrought and accepted fibre of American politics. If the temple of our republic shall ever fall, they will " still live" above the ground, like those great foundation-stones in ancient ruins which remain in lonely grandeur, unburied in the dust that over all else springs to turf, and make men wonder from what rare quarry and by what mighty force they came. To Webster almost more than to any other man, — nay, at this distance, and in the generous spirit of this occasion, it is hard to discriminate among the lustrous names which now cluster at the gates of heaven as golden bars mass the west at sunset, — yet to Webster, especially of them all, is it due that to-day, wherever a son of the United States, at home or abroad, " beholds the gorgeous ensign of the republic, now known and honored throughout the earth, still full high advanced, its arms and trophies streaming in their original lustre, not a stripe erased or polluted, not a single star obscured," he can utter a prouder boast than " Civis Romanus sum." For he can say, I am an American citizen.

WENDELL PHILLIPS.

At a Memorial Meeting in the Congregational Church, Washington, D. C., February 22, 1884.

EXCEPT amid the affectionate associations of his native place and home, no spot could be more fitting in which to honor the memory of Wendell Phillips than the capital of the nation whose one great blot his fiery eloquence burnt out. No day could be more appropriate than the birthday of Washington, whose victories for American independence were but half won till this zealot preached the crusade that crowned them at Appomattox. No body of men could more fitly gather around his open grave and bedew it with their grateful tears than those who represent the race whose shackles he turned into garlands amid which they now lay him to rest. Well may the "Goddess of Liberty" on yonder dome strain her tear-dimmed eyes to the north, listening to catch once more the thrill of a voice, but for which she might have towered this day only as a brazen lie. Of the great names that in these latter days of the republic stand for its redemption from crime against itself, and for its perfected consecration to human freedom, his blazes out among the foremost few. Upon the earlier anti-slavery heights, he gives place to Garrison alone. And when I remember that in my own honored commonwealth — in Massachusetts, star of the North — flamed these two immortal spirits, and so many others who clustered around them, I cannot refrain from joining my voice with yours in honoring this one of them which has latest taken its flight back to God, who gave it.

In the case of most great men, even of those who suggest their limitations least, we speak of the steps, the milestones, the dates, and events of their career. But to recite those of Wendell Phillips seems out of place. His was the force, not of the stream, which gathers volume as it flows, and pours its resistless flood in a steady current, marking its beneficence by the fair cities it builds along its banks; nor of the fire which, under the mastery of law, turns the mighty wheels of the machinery and onward locomotion of the age; but rather of the wind that bloweth where it listeth, now in the exquisite music of a zephyr over an æolian harp strung with human sympathies and graces, and now in the sweep of a tornado, smiting every rotten trunk to the earth, and making even the sturdy and honest oak bend before its storm. His was not the service of Lincoln or Andrew in executive station, of Sumner or Stevens in Congress, of Grant or Sherman in the field, adapting means to successive steps of advance, and working through the best agencies at hand to achieve the best results possible; but it was the service of the torch that is flung at large to kindle the conflagration at the beginning, and, whatever burns, to keep it flaming on. He was no patient ox, toiling under the yoke and at his load. He was often rather the goad-stick which pricked those who were dragging burdens, in the homely carriage of which he was less serviceable than were those he prodded. He was a man of inspirations, not of affairs. His not to make or interpret or execute the law; his not the equipment for that work; but his to quicken the public sentiment of which law is the expression and force. When its formulation and fruit had come for others, when they had encamped content, this pillar of cloud by day and of fire by night was already in the nebulous distance, beckoning them to a new lead and advance. Not the safest guide in the slow and sure economies of material welfare, he was rather the prophet of the people's conscience, the poet of their noblest impulses.

It seems as if when, in Faneuil Hall nearly fifty years ago, in his early youth, he leaped into the arena for human rights, he flung aside every incumbrance of ordinary growth toward the achievement of a plan of life, and streamed at once into flame. Born a patrician, he was such a tribune of the people as Rome never dreamed of, who knew no law, only the law of their enlargement and of their broadening, and of their equal rights of life, liberty, and the pursuit of happiness. With the genius of a scholar, touched with the fine culture of letters, his mind itself a classic, he scorned the noble avenues of the statesman, the useful walks of political service, the delights of literature, all of which lay at his hand, and gave himself to the passionate impulses of a great human charity, — to the cause of the oppressed, the enslaved, the poor, the down-trodden, and the friendless. Into the great anti-slavery cause and conflict he rode, — a warrior whose sword was to flash and whose voice was to ring till the last battlefield was won. To that cause he gave all except that exquisite loyalty to her who sat at his hearth, which, faithful even unto death, is now as grateful and sweet to the American people as the white leaves of a flower or the tenderest heart-beat in a poet's song. For that cause he sacrificed all, enduring, as it is impossible now to realize, obloquy and shame, hissing and hate. No man is altogether the master of his own character or inclination, and it is not, perhaps, to be wondered at that, from the terrific ordeal through which in those days Phillips went,

and from the wounds he then received at the hands of his
own caste, came something of the spirit that never after
could quite reconcile itself with the ranks that later were
sincerely ready to do him justice. A victim of injustice,
there were times when he did injustice. And perhaps
there could be no more complete tribute to his character,
than that in his later years, as well as now in the halo of
his death, his eloquence, his singleness and purity of purpose, his lofty integrity, and his great work were the ac-
knowledgment and pride of all his fellow citizens alike;
and that to question his opinions was never to accuse the
disinterested fervor of his convictions and ideas. Ah
with what admiration — it seems but yesterday in the
streets of Boston — we looked, as we saw above the throng
that commanding and high-spirited face, never quite free
from its scorn of conscious superiority! We turned to
gaze upon him when he had passed, — that higher-bred
and more beautiful Puritan Apollo, whose tongue was his
lute, and whose swift shaft was winged with the immortal fire of liberty. A city-full and a nation-full honor
him. He has his reward in the praise even of those who
differed from him most; and he has his reward — and to
him it is the sweetest — in the tears and gratitude of
thousands in humble life, to whom his name is as that
thought of a friend, which to many, alas, is so rare, yet
by every human being is so longed for. There are humble homes of plain living, but of high thinking, in
my own New England, under the shadow of Plymouth
Rock, along the sea and among the farms, to which my
heart turns as I speak, and in which are men and women,
peers of his courage and humanity, though not of his gifts
and fame, who remember and mourn this leader, whose
eloquence and fire kindled their youth with enthusiasm

for human rights, and who endeared himself to them by sharing with them the persecution of the opinions of that time. There are oppressed peoples in foreign lands who lament an advocate and champion of the larger and sweeter liberty of which they dream, and which he yearned to see them enjoy. There are five million citizens of our own, to whom and to whose descendants he will be as a deliverer, like him who led the children of Israel out of their bondage.

As in his own career Phillips disdained the ordinary steps and methods of influence and growth, so in any estimate of him all the ordinary modes of analysis and criticism are useless. What are his errors in economical science; what are his mistaken estimates of men and measures; what are his bitter injustices to patriots as true as himself; what are his rashnesses of judgment, looked at in the light of his lofty consecration to his fellow men and of that absolute innocence of any purpose of self-aggrandizement, which you felt as distinctly in his character as you heard the music in his voice, and which separated him so utterly from the mouthing demagogues whose self-seeking is as patent as their roar? What are all these, if these there were, except as they were the incidentals, not the essentials, of a nature that went to its mark with the relentless stroke of the lightning, and, had it not been the lightning, would have been nothing? Our glorious summer days sometimes breed, even in the very rankness of their opulence, enervating and unhealthy weaknesses. The air is heavy. Its breath poisons the blood; the pulse of nature is sluggish and mean. Then come the tempest and the thunder. So was it in the body politic, whether the plague was slavery or whatever wrong; whether it was weakness in men of high degree or tyranny over men of low estate; whether it was the curse of the grog-shop, or the iron hand of the despot at home or abroad, — so it was that like the lightning Phillips flashed and struck. The scorching, hissing bolt rent the air, now here, now there. From heaven to earth, now wild at random, now straight it shot. It streamed across the sky. It leaped in broken links of a chain of fire. It sometimes fell with reckless indiscrimination alike on the just and on the unjust. It sometimes smote the innocent as well as blasted the guilty. But when the tempest was over, there was a purer and a fresher spirit in the air, and a sweeter health. Louder than the thunder, mightier than the wind, the earthquake, or the fire, a still small voice spake in the public heart, and the public conscience woke.

GEORGE F. EDMUNDS.

Nominating Speech in the Republican Presidential
Convention at Chicago, June 5, 1884.

Mr. President and Fellow Delegates, — We are
here to discharge a trust. Let us remember that we are
to account for it hereafter. I appeal to the unimpassioned
judgment of this convention. I appeal from the excitement of this vast concourse to the afterthought of the
firesides of the people. And remembering that an American audience never fails in fair play, I appeal even at
this late hour for an opportunity for brave little Vermont.

The Republican party commands to-day the confidence
of the country. It need not invoke its record of twenty-
five years, for that is the common knowledge and admiration of the world. It need not appeal to its principles,
for those are the very foundation of the marvelous progress and prosperity of this great republic. There only
needs that, in its candidate, in the simple elements of his
personal and public character, it furnish a guarantee of
its continued fidelity to itself. There only needs that it
respond to the instinct of the people. That done, its
triumph in the coming presidential election is as sure as
the coming of election day. But, gentlemen, that instinct
must be obeyed. It represents a demand which is as in-
exorable as fate itself. It recognizes the merits and the
services of all the candidates before us. It obtrudes no
word of depreciation for any of them. It cares little for
issues of expediency or preferences of personal or party

liking. But by that awful voice of the people which is as the voice of God, it sets an imperative standard of its choice and bids us rise to that or fall.

We are convened, therefore, in behalf of no man. The country and the party are greater than the fortunes or the interests of any man, however dear or honored. We are here as Republicans, and yet brave and broad enough not to be here in the interest of the Republican party alone. Even in this tumultuous excitement we feel that, charged with the most sacred responsibilities that can fall upon representatives of the people, we are here in the interests of the people, and all the people — of the country and the whole country. We are here to select for President a man from our own ranks, indeed, but a man whose record and character, whose tested service, whose tried incorruptibility, whose unscathed walk through the storms and fires of public life, whose approved wisdom equal to every emergency, whose recognized capacity to put a firm, safe hand upon the helm, and whose hold upon the confidence of the people, make him not our choice for them, but their choice for themselves. He must be one who will command their undivided support. Not merely brilliant qualities, on the one hand, or meritorious qualities, on the other, are enough. He must be of the staying qualities of the sturdiest American character. He must represent no wing or faction of the party, but the whole of it. He must be one who will hold every Republican to his cordial allegiance, who will rally indifference and independence even into aroused conviction and an earnest front on our line ; one who will stand for every beat that ever throbbed in the national heart for humanity, freedom, conscience, and reform ; one who will stand for whatever has been honest and of good report in our national history — for whatever has made for economy, financial wisdom, clean politics, and the integrity of national life. And, above all, he must be one whose name will carry in the coming canvass that sense of security to which, at each presidential election, the country turns as the very rock of salvation. Such a man, honest and capable, will first master the sober judgment and approval of the people, and thenceforward stir them to the only enthusiasm, my friends, that counts, and that is the enthusiasm of public confidence. And then on election day, conscious where their safety lies, the irresistible uprising of the people, like the mighty inrolling of an ocean tide, will sweep him, never fear, into the highest seat of your public service.

That is the measure and demand, not of a party, but of the country. Meet it, and you have done your work and won your victory in advance. Respond here and now to this instinct of the people, and they will take care of the result. The standard is high, but the candidate I name rises to it. If there be an ideal American citizen in the best sense, it is he. You know, the people know, that his character, his ability, his worth, his courage are as recognized and familiar as a household word. Calumny dare not assail him, and, if it dare, recoils as from a galvanic shock. Against no other candidate can less be said than against him. For no other candidate can more.

I stand here, Mr. President, honored though I stood alone, with the duty of presenting his name to this convention. But it is not I, it is not the State nor the delegates whom I here represent, who present that name to you. It is presented by uncounted numbers of our fellow citizens, good men and true, all over this land, who only await his nomination to spring to the swift and hearty work of his election. It is presented by an intelligent

press, from Maine to California, representing a healthy
public sentiment and an advanced public demand. It is
the name of one whose letter of acceptance of an unso-
licited honor will constitute all the machinery he will
have put into its procurement. It is a name which in
itself is a guarantee of inflexible honesty in government,
and of the best and wisest cabinet the country can afford,
— no man in it greater than its head. It is a guarantee
of appointments to office, fit, clean, and disinterested all
the way through, — a guarantee of an administration
which I believe, and which in your hearts you know, will
realize, not only at home, but abroad, the very highest
conceptions of American statesmanship. It is a name,
too, which will carry over all the land a grateful feeling
of serenity and security like the benignant promise of a
"perfect day in June." It will be as wholesome and
refreshing as the green mountains of the native State of
him who bears it. Their summits tower not higher than
his worth; their foundations are not firmer than his
convictions and truth; the verdant and prolific slopes
that grow great harvests at their feet are not richer than
the fruitage of his long and lofty labors in the service
of his country. Honest and capable, unexceptionable
and fit, the best and most available, the very staunchest
of the old Republican guard, the most unflinching of
American patriots, with the kindly heart of a courteous
gentleman, as well as the robust and rugged mind of a
great statesman, not more sternly just in the halls of Congress than tender in that sanctity of the American heart,
the American home, a man of no class, no caste, no pre-
tense, but a man of the people, East, West, North, South,
because a representative of their homeliest, plainest,
and best characteristics! Massachusetts, enthusiastically

leaping her own borders, commends and nominates him to this great Republican convention as the man it seeks, as a man of its instinctive and honest choice, as the one man whom its constituents everywhere will hail with one unbroken shout, not only of satisfaction, but of relief.

Gentlemen, I nominate as the Republican candidate for the next President of the United States the Honorable, aye, the honorable George F. Edmunds of Vermont.

RESPONSE

I OUGHT to thank you, Mr. Chairman, for assigning
to me a toast of such remote reference as " Forefathers'
Day." Some of us in New England feel just at this time
like going as far back as possible for any cause of victorious glorification. You here in New York may knock over
our modern fetiches, but you cannot reach the chip on the
shoulder of our Pilgrim forefather. We celebrate to-
night the day of his landing two hundred and sixty-four
years ago. I suppose I shall startle nobody if I say it
was a great event. Indeed, I have heard gentlemen intimate — once even at this loyal table, though I am bound
to say it was the envious utterance of a Knickerbocker —
that they would admit its greatness if we who glory in it
would not argue and assert it so loudly and so often. As
Judge Hoar said of the malcontents in the recent political campaign, if they needs must go out they need n't
slam the door so hard ; so these suggest that, if we must
praise the Pilgrim, we need not do it in such a way as to
make comparison with the ancestors of other people not
altogether agreeable. Our modest answer is that we cannot help it if the superiority in that respect is on our side.
We cannot help it, but we can be merciful. We should
remember that even an Athenian tired of hearing Aris-
tides always called the Just. In our case, also, I doubt
not the lessons we draw get to be somewhat monotonous

and heavy. It was a wise little girl — my own — who
said, when a good old lady offered to tell her a nice story,
she would like to hear it if she were not pretty sure there
would be the usual moral at the end of it.

And there is another reason why one should hesitate to
pay the tribute of your society to the Pilgrims. The
eagle has been let loose so often that his wings are a little
shaky. I admit that I ought to respond. I represent, to
put it mildly, the foremost Congressional District in the
United States, before which Boston and this magnificent
conglomerate which you call New York pale their intellectual fires, for in it is Plymouth Rock. My direct
ancestor, too, Thomas Clark, who came over in the third
Pilgrim ship, the Anne, in 1623, resides on Burial Hill
in an humble one-story basement, and his is one of the
three or four original gravestones still standing there. I
have no doubt that he now regards himself as well repaid
for the hardships of his earthly pilgrimage, when he reflects that his grandson in a remote generation draws an
indifferently earned salary from the treasury of the mighty
empire he helped to found. I trust that I, at my end of
the line, feel a due sense of filial gratitude to him for his
labors and perils in that behalf, when monthly I draw
that humble stipend. Indeed, I sometimes think we do
not sufficiently appreciate what our fathers did for us in
that respect. We are too apt to limit our appreciation to
certain commonplaces of fundamental moral principles, of
great lumbering planks of civil and religious liberty, and
of education, with its three R's, Reading, 'Riting, and
'Rithmetic, which have recently been corrupted into that
more striking, perhaps, but certainly unfortunate allit-
eration which an illiterate preacher lately misquoted as
" Rum, Romanism, and Rebellion."

We should go further, and extend our appreciation to the homelier but closer-coming blessings of the Government they founded, with its public trough of one hundred and fifty thousand compartments, more or less, its udders of emolumental patronage flowing with milk and soap, and its warm official hearth-fires, where, after half the boys have toasted their shins for four years, the other half demand to come in from their dance on the cold pavement and toast theirs, when, as in the recent electoral contest, one good party is turned down and out, and another, which has yet to earn, as let us trust it will earn, its laudatory adjective, is brought to the top by a mysterious dispensation which the same preacher, mourning defeat, yet dutifully resigned, meaning to quote correctly and reverently, but unsuccessful in the attempt, might have called the dispensation of " an All-wise but Unscrupulous Providence."

Yes, I hesitate at your toast. I am like a neophyte who scrapes the bow across a violin and makes it an instrument of torture. I think of the master who, nestling it tenderly beneath his cheek, as if it and he were one, touches the sweet chords of however ancient a melody, and, rapt himself, enwraps our listening souls in memories that by turns stir us to heroism or melt us to tears. The poetry of life is its crown, — that exaltation of sentiment, of religious feeling, of heroic endeavor, of immortal aspiration, which make life, when at its best, a poem. And never since Moses led the children of Israel toward the promised land has there been such an epic as the voyage of the Mayflower and the landing at Plymouth. If the master of a nobler instrument than the violin could sweep the chords of that great song, he would wake no dirge or lament, but the melody of the universal heart, the spirit of loftiest vision, and would indeed by turns stir to heroism and melt to tears. Ah, how narrowly and mistakenly we limit those men and women of the Mayflower when we shrivel them with the winter blast of a December day, harden them into the solemnity of ascetics, or think of them as refugees from personal annoyances.

While they were, as some one has said, "neither Puritans nor persecutors," they were, as is too rarely said, something far more, — they were poets, they were idealists. They were glad children of the light, seeking for "more light." They were warm with youth and adventure, yet transcendentalists mounting a new heaven. Read the compact drawn in the cabin of the Mayflower, — read in it the statement of the object of their coming, and say where has the genius of bard or prophet struck such a strain as those words expressive of their purpose: "For the glory of God and advancement of the Christian faith and honor of our King and countrie!" Here is no wretched care for personal interests, no craven thought of flight or escape from petty persecutions, no whining solicitude for individual fortune, but the high soul of men who "plant a colony" and found an empire for nothing less than the glory of God, the advancement of their faith, the honor of their country. This is not the fuss of a house-moving, but the sublimity of inspired poetic genius, as it is also the consummation of statesmanship and patriotism. To them the coast, which Mrs. Hemans has so extravagantly belied, and which is really as gentle as a post-election editorial, was the fringe of God's paradise; its wild grapes and red berries and running vines, and its mayflowers, peeping in spring-time through its moss, were the bursting glory of a better than tropical luxuriance.

Do you think any ignobler spirit than the poet's wrought this vision, or would have kept them there when the first winter struck down half their number, and, standing on the hill, they watched the sails of the returning Mayflower fade out in the light of an April day? You sneer at their psalm-singing and think complacently of a shrieking opera. That is because you know only of psalms sung through the nose. They sung psalms, but they were songs of high cheer and were their melody and outburst, — not sombre strains, but peace, supremacy, and content, in which mingled the fireside voices of pure women and happy children. You think they shrank from the savage and heard his whoop in their dreams. That is because you are timid and live in cities. To them the Indian's first word was "Welcome, Englishmen." With now and then a rare and wholesome correction, he lived in peace with them for generations; and tradition has it that two children of the forest begged to be buried at the feet of Bradford, and now lie with him on Burial Hill. Fear! Standish, panting for the elbow-room of perfect freedom, and separating himself from the rest, even as they had all separated themselves from their English homes, dwelt apart across the channel in the grandeur of his solitary Duxbury realm.

You think there was no softness or merriment in their lives; but you forget that John Alden looked in the eyes of Priscilla Mullens and walked with her in the "lovers' lanes" of the "forest primeval." You forget to catch the laugh with which Mary Chilton, ancestress of Copley and Lyndhurst, waded from the boat to the shore, — first woman of them all to put her dainty foot on American soil. You forget the romance of Alice Southworth's coming later over from England to wed the young widower

Bradford, who had loved her when a girl among the English hawthorns. You forget that the Pilgrim's was the first New England home, — God bless it! — the same rural home that you and I came from, over whose doors the roses grew in our youth, fading there, but fresh and fragrant always here in our hearts. You picture a rigid ecclesiastical tyranny. You forget that there was among them no ordained minister — happy parish! — and that Brewster, who led their devotions, had been a man of courts, a bearer of Queen Elizabeth's dispatches. You pity them for a life of more than provincial narrowness of affairs. You forget that Winslow, a man of the world and of travel in foreign parts, was an ambassador and diplomat, negotiating treaties with Massasoit; that he was four times sent over sea to England — what man at this board can equal that record — to arrange the relations of the old world with the new; and that he died in the service of Cromwell, superintending the invasion of the West Indies.

Picture Governor Bradford, in his long cloak, marching to meeting of a Sunday morning, flanked on one side by Brewster, the saint, and on the other by Standish, the soldier. Compared with that, what is the Fourth of March Inauguration of a President, flanked on both sides by expectants? Think of the stately excursions of the Pilgrims through the virgin forest; their quieting of Indian troubles; their making of history where we make cloth and leather; their adventurous sailing expeditions to explore Massachusetts Bay, the wind fresh, the waves rippling in the sunshine, the freedom of a new world in their hearts, and anon opening on their gaze the mouths of the Charles and the Mystic, and the three hills of Boston, silent then, but never silent since. Think

of their discreet squelching of the Independents, who
at that time were rioting at Merry Mount in Quincy,
and who, by the way, still infest that vicinity even to
this day, as my own imperiled political scalp bears
witness.

These Pilgrims were men who were greater than the
restrictions of English life ; who were broader than the
huckstering and traffic of their Holland tarrying-place ;
and who, therefore, fled from both, gasping for larger
breath.   They were no narrow Puritans who vexed themselves over questions of method or form or discipline in
the church.   They broke altogether from the church itself,
were separatists, and set up their own establishment for
themselves and for the New World, — themselves an evangel of religious and civil liberty.   No Puritans they,
intolerant of another's faith, but great-hearted liberals,
welcoming Roger Williams, the original mugwump, when,
driven from Salem, he came to them, but found his own
sweet will so dull, that, like a true mugwump, his restless
soul soon wearied of its own freedom, and he returned
to the intolerant fold that had driven him forth, as mug-
wumps sooner or later always do return, and as intolerant
folds sooner or later always do take them back.   Sympathy for the hardships of the Pilgrim fathers !   They
would laugh at you.   They never dreamed of yielding or
of going or looking back.   Why, it were worth a thousand years, a cycle of Cathay, to have breathed the air
with them, to have put one's name to that cabin compact,
to have planted that colony.   Compare their great enterprise and range with selling stocks in Wall Street, with
the strife of bulls and bears, with winning or losing a
Presidential race, and in either case being trampled on
and run over by fifty million howling American citizens,

clergymen included, or with achieving the fame of figuring in the colored prints of Puck or Jingo!

Truth is, our lives are the rich responsive answer to their own. Theirs was a pæan. They were idealists, poets, seers, but it was that germinating and rich idealism which flowers out in the world's glory and beneficence. If it was poetry, it is a poetry that lives after them, in a larger vitality and range. Its music is not a far-off strain. It is not confined to a stone's-throw from the rock on which they set foot. It rolls across a continent from sea to sea. It explores the frozen zone, and just now wooes and wins the Nicaraguan Isthmus. It is poetry, indeed, but the poetry of industry, of growth, of school and farm, of shop and ship and car. You hear it now in the hum of ten thousand mills, in the trip of a hundred thousand ham-mers, in the bustle of myriad exchanges, in the voice of a mighty people who are a mighty people, and will be mightier yet, because and so far as they are true to the courage of the Pilgrim Fathers, to their lofty stride and aspiration, to their superiority over fortune and the dust, to their foundations of education and the home, and to their consecration of themselves to the glory of God, the advancement of faith and the honor of their country.

Forefathers' Day! We have no day that is not Fore-fathers' Day. Our national Independence is their sepa-ratism. Standish is the common prototype of Grant and Sherman. Whatever is wholesome in our social life is the effluence of their homes. Our constitutional liberty and our constitutional law are the consummate flower of their compact. I doubt if there be to-day a radical footprint that may not trace itself to them; and many an economic and industrial result is an issue from their good sense and honest labor. Our absorption of the progressive elements of other nationalities and religions, illustrated by the recent election of an Irish-born Catholic mayor of the very New England metropolis, is philosophically the outgrowth of the liberalism with which they welcomed all men on the common ground of good citizenship.

This great democracy of ours, the broadest-based and securest government in the world, self-sufficient, self-sustaining, self-restrained, and developing new capacity to meet every new necessity and demand of its own stupendous and startling growth, is only the expansion of their own democracy. Let us do our duty by it as faithfully as they did theirs. Doing that, let us await its destiny as calmly as did they, assured, as they were, that liberty is better than repression; that liberty, making and obeying its own laws, is God; and that unless man, made in His image, is a failure, the self-government of a free and educated people, whatever its occasional vicissitudes, will not and cannot fail.

I do not know that in cold blood I could stand by all I have said concerning the Pilgrim Fathers; but do we not owe them something more than a half-disguised sneer or that patronizing crust of sympathy which we toss to a shivering beggar? This is not altogether a rhetorical interrogation. I believe — just this once — in the Methodist custom of passing the contribution-box, provided I hold it and the other fellows fill it. At Plymouth, on one of its hills, overlooking the ocean, is a noble monument of granite. To our provincial eyes it is a bigger thing than the Washington Monument. The pedestal is forty-five feet high. On that stands, towering thirty-six feet higher, a colossal statue of Faith, the generous but modest gift of a donor unknown till his death. Her eyes look toward the sea. Forever she beholds upon its waves the incoming Mayflower. She sees the Pilgrims land. They vanish, but she, the monument of their faith, remains and tells their story to the world. This our generation, too, shall pass away, and its successors for centuries to come; but she will stand, and, overlooking our forgotten memory, will still speak of them and of their foundation of the republic on the Plymouth rocks of Faith, Liberty, Law, Morality, and Education.

Around the pedestal at her feet, statues of the two last sit in kindred granite. Those of Liberty and Law are yet lacking, as they were not lacking in the temple which the Pilgrims built. What a happy thing it would be if you, the New England Society of New York City, contributing to this monumental group raised to their honor, should to Faith, Education, and Morality, add Law or Liberty, or both; or, rather than permit any favoritism in such an inestimable privilege, if you should add one and your sister society in Brooklyn add the other.

EULOGY

On Senator Austin F. Pike, of New Hampshire, in the
House of Representatives at Washington, February
23, 1887.

I do not rise, Mr. Speaker, to enlarge upon Senator
Pike's political or professional career. That matter is
sufficiently touched by those more familiar with it. In
that respect it is enough for me that his life was, as has
been portrayed, one of faithful service and perfect integrity, and that honors were never paid to a man of more
genuine worth or honest record.

I rise rather because, during his senatorial residence in
Washington, we lived under the same roof. Almost
daily I saw him, and was in converse with him, and I came
to know something of the deeper inspirations and treasures
of his life. To the world at large our lives here are lives
of official routine. But to ourselves, as the days go by,
bringing us closer together, familiarizing us with each
other's faces, with the grasp of each other's hands, and
with the sound of each other's voices, suddenly it comes
that we are no longer perfunctory associates, but friends
and companions. There is in each, indeed, the conventional discharge of his duty, but beneath that and far
more impressive on our consciousness is the recognition of
qualities that mark not so much the statesman as the
man. Out of the unrelieved mass of the representative
population which we face when we enter here, there steadily emerges on us in clearer outline, each day we stay,
traits of individual character, personalities of individual

men, the opening of the treasures of the individual human
heart, and the expression of those affections, tastes, ambitions, devotions, purposes, or ideals which make each one
of us a distinct individuality, yet subtly intimate with
every other. And when one goes from us, say what you
will, recite never so eloquently the story of his public
achievement, the one sincere chord that thrills in the
breasts of those who remain is that of the regard he had
won in their hearts. And the measure of that regard is
the measure of response to his memory.

In this respect I recall Senator Pike with a reverent
tenderness I cannot express. From the time we both entered the Forty-eighth Congress I recall meeting, almost
daily each session, a sweet, grave, benignant face, more like
the picture of Rufus Choate — a graduate of the same
Granite State, prolific of great men — than any other
that occurs to me. I recall a gentle, almost pathetic,
smile, significant of the sweet and gentle spirit from
which it sprang, — a man ripe in years, delicate in health,
yet suggestive of something of a certain rugged New England plainness, intent on duty, going about his work in
the simplest and most exemplary way, and absolutely free
from all entanglements of selfish strategic manœuvre.
He had not been long enough in the Senate to take, if
ever he would have taken, foremost part in its greater
questions and debates. But there was the most diligent,
painstaking, careful, and thorough attention to the details
of the cumulative work which the chairmanship of his
laborious committee threw upon him. To this work he
brought not only patience and assiduity, but a sound judgment, an intelligent comprehension, and the trained mind
of a good lawyer and a wise man. Of such a character it
may seem a little thing in the way of eulogy, but to me

who was near him it is a very grateful thing to recall the
simple genuineness of the man's nature, — even the kind
tones of his voice, his encouraging interest in younger
men, and the gracious words to children, which, together
with a certain benignity in his face, drew them to him.
It is a grateful thing to remember that among all who
came into companionship with him there was an unspoken
but unquestioned recognition of him as a true, honest, good
man, with all that those fundamental terms mean ; that to
all who came to him in his official relation, no matter
how humble the applicant or small the petition, there
was a genuine response ; and that if one may touch the
sacred altar of the domestic circle, he was its very benediction. By reason of an affection of the heart his life
was continually trembling in the most sensitive balance.
And if I dwell on these personal traits, it is because he
seemed to me to be conscious all this time that the angel
of death walked at his side, ready at any moment to take
his hand and lead him away ; and that with that consciousness there came to him not only the brave spirit of resignation, but the braver spirit of doing his duty to the last,
to the last letting only sunshine radiate from his face, only
helpfulness from his hand. When our friends die, we
say God rest their souls. But God rested his while he
yet lived in the very face of death. No soldier ever faced
it in the sudden and soon-over flash of battle more hero-
ically than did he, with a serenity that was proof against
its more appalling, because constant and silent, close impendence.

It was the fitness of poetic justice, that not here in
Washington, but in his own New Hampshire home, death
claimed him — amid the incomparable beauty and glory
of the New Hampshire autumn sunshine — in the open

air of that paradise of mountain and forest and lake and
farm and field to which every New Hampshire heart is
loyal, and on the acres won and cultivated by his own
hand.   There, as peacefully as his own blameless life had
run, as serenely as his kind face beamed, came the end.
The angel, who is even tenderer and gentler than her
sister Sleep, had indeed walked at his side so long that he
recognized her as the blessed angel of man's succor and
peace.   She had waited till their walk that bright day,
over the pleasant fields and under the blue sky, gave the
opportunity happiest for her and for him.   Then she
gathered her arms about him.   His head fell upon her
shoulder even as he went.   And lo! he was at rest in the
mansions of his Father's house.

ADDRESS

BEFORE THE AMERICAN UNITARIAN ASSOCIATION IN MUSIC HALL,
BOSTON, MAY 29, 1877.

I LIKE this idea of missionary work right here at home, and I care very little under what banner it proceeds. I am not much afraid of what our various sects denominate, in everybody except themselves, false doctrine, if only it be honestly entertained, and if there is candor enough to reject it when its falsity is made apparent. It will be time for any of us to call another's doctrine false when we can ourselves with any confidence assert that our own is true. False and true are relative terms, and I shall probably know very little about the false till I have arrived at the absolutely true. Let us remember that the false is often a lame step towards the true. A grand thing, indeed, it would be, in a catholic and hopeful spirit, to regard all reaching of the human intelligence and soul as a growth along the whole line towards the truth. Let us not despise or dread honest and inquiring error. How have the sciences of medicine and astronomy, how have the progresses of social life, the causes of education, of health, of legislation, been advanced except by deduction from error and the hard discipline of blunder!

I preface this because I regard our mission as only a mission, not an end; as a very humble, but intelligent and fearless means, which in God's providence is doing God's work and seeking God's truth, along with other means, some better perhaps, some certainly not so good,

and all poor compared with future possibilities of Christianity. It is a mission fit here and now, because the
mission of our liberal faith has always been not so much
to the ignorance of remote heathen as to intelligence and
common sense and spiritual attainment like those of this
rare and excellent New England community. It has been
a twofold mission, and I am not sure that in one of its
two directions its work, as a distinctive work of its own,
is not approaching completion. For a century, more or
less, it has been a very ploughshare in the hard and bitter
soil of a severe theology, which hid the smiles of a tender
Father always behind the frown of an offended and
averted Deity, which robbed human nature of its worth
and dignity, and which substituted the skeleton of a tech-
nical and complicated scheme of injustice for the warm
life of the domesticity of man with God. On all this it
has let in sunlight and gladness and cheer. It has mel-
lowed even the shadow of death with the tints of a golden
sunset of promise. It has left its imprint not more in its
own ranks than in ranks outside its own. Its results are
hardly more Channing and Hale and Clarke than Brooks
and Stanley. Its influence is not more patent in the fruitful graft of the Methodist Collyer than in the earnest
work of the revivalist Moody, who seems almost of another faith than that of the revivalists of fifty years ago.
I want no more generous and comfortable atmosphere
than pervades the churches of so many of our neighbors,
who differ from us to-day less in spirit than in name, and
from whose number our own ministry is now and then
supplied with many of its shining lights.

It has been a good work, — that of our liberal faith in
this direction ; and, may be, in this direction, its most
effective labor is done. It is not for us to say that the

time is not near when it will itself no longer guide the
advance, but in its turn follow some brighter torch, some
more incisive lead. Be that as it may, the other element
of its mission it can never exhaust. Its crusade against
narrowness of dogma over, the better and endless work of
being a live, vitalizing, inspiring, practical, constant, per-
meating spring and flow of Christian character and love
and faith in the world should absorb its endeavors. Science, scholarship, brains, will take care of the letter and the
doctrine; let us have now the full measure of the spirit
and the life. Let us preach the sweetness of faith and
duty, more of the soul of Jesus, more of the spiritual
exaltation that lifts the conduct, the thought, the hope,
the act. Would there were more divinity schools turning
out classes of young men all richly and mainly educated
in spiritual grace, as our academies turn out boys drilled
in Latin exercises! Would that our churches might glow
more with the warmth of religious kindling, echoing less
with the puzzles of the modern schoolmen! Would that
the hearts of men and women might be touched, their lives
guided, so that Christian civilization should be not the
husk of a euphuism, but the full corn in the ear of Christian living; and that we could feel assured that *our* faith
were indeed making us better and holier; moulding our
relations; guiding our walk; entering into our business,
and even our politics; directing our education; reforming
our reforms; enlightening our treatment of the criminal;
attacking our intemperance; sanctifying and spiritual-
izing our ambitions; making our religion not a form, a
habit, a convenience, but something bountiful and large
and immanent; making our churches places of worship,
and training us, through Christ's sweet example, into
loving, trusting, obedient, and pious children of God, —

blessed because gentle in spirit; meek; hungering and
thirsting after righteousness; merciful; pure in heart;
peacemakers; and persecuted, if at all, for righteousness'
sake! From my soul I believe we have nothing so good
as the gospel of Jesus. Our church, having dissipated
shadow and gloom, must not and will not fall short of the
substance. That substance is that gospel, — the life, history, words, character, example, faith, and, more than all,
the principles of Jesus, which all appeal to the heart of
humanity, as no abstraction can; and by clinging to
which, and dwelling on which, and preaching which, and
endearing which, other churches reach men as sometimes
we do not. Let us, too, throw out one more anchor in
this same deep and restful haven. Not an iota less of
intelligence and reason and truth, but a worldfull and a
heartfull of the spirit of him who through his own has
linked our souls so palpably to the divine soul, that the
avenue to the Father's love and benediction seems to lie
straight through the tender heart of the Son.

RESPONSE

For the Commonwealth at the Dinner of the Ancient and Honorable Artillery Company, at Faneuil Hall, June 5, 1882.

I DO not forget, Mr. Commander and gentlemen, that I am here to-day not only as a civil magistrate, — an office which, of course, any of you might have, could you spare the time, — but also as an honorary member of this ancient and honorable company, — a position which I share with Wales, and with Wales only. By Wales it is unnecessary to say that I refer, not to our gallant new brigadier and commissioner of police, but a gentleman across the water, who, while I, more fortunate, feast at this sumptuous board, is obliged to content himself, for the present, with an Irish stew. Bearing this relation to you, no word shall escape my lips that lightly speaks of your fame, your bearing, or your merits as a military organization. From the top of the New England pyramid, almost two centuries and a half look down on you to-day, and do you honor. A saucy press may point its inky finger; the citizen who never buckled a sword to his side, except in time of war, may wag his head; but, while thrones and custom-house officials totter, while men may come and men may go, the Ancient and Honorable Artillery Company flows on forever; and its morning drum-beat, following the fife, and keeping company with your graceful step, circles, if not the earth, at least its hub, with one continuous and unbroken strain of the martial airs of Yankee Massachusetts. As we marched hither, and I looked into the upper

windows of the buildings that line the way, I could not
forget that the tired sewing-girl ceased singing the " Song
of the Shirt," that the laboring man wiped the sweat from
his honest brow, that the organ-grinder stopped his tune,
that the newsboy stood motionless, as they watched your
march, — perhaps their only amusement for the whole
year.

Age cannot wither your appetites, nor custom stale
your infinite variety. The years have fallen from you
like the sunbeams from the helmet of Hector. Still the
same defiant march that neither storm nor tempest, nor
discipline by land or sea, nor anything but actual service
can retard. Still the same artistically irregular step and
wheel. Still the same familiar handling of musket and
sword so characteristic of men who carry them only once
a year, as you have carried them for two hundred and
forty-four years, yet never have shed a drop of blood, never
terrified wife or child, — except your own. Still the same
picturesque variety of uniform which finds itself rivaled
nowhere else except upon the stage of the opera. And
yet, if you will allow me to say so, I trust the time will
never come when the Ancient and Honorable Artillery
Company will wear an unbroken uniform. All pleasantry
aside, there is not a citizen that sees you marching through
the streets who does not see in the variety of your uni-
forms the representation of our martial organizations which
went through the flame and smoke of war, or who does
not recognize that beneath them beat hearts which twenty
years ago were, and which twenty years hence, should
we need them, will still be ready to fight for the honor
of Massachusetts. You have also shown every faithful
citizen of the Commonwealth that, while too busy to serve
in the narrow confines of the jury-box, he may serve her
in another field better for himself and possibly for her.

You have inaugurated a system of civil service which reforms even the young reformers, putting promotion not upon the rock of political influence, not upon the accident of merit, but as your later commanders unanimously tell us, upon the proud distinction of personal beauty.

When this morning, in your line of march, you saluted the venerable State House, you saluted an edifice a century and a half younger than yourselves. Your very years, while they compel you to put the example of good conduct before your fellow citizens, entitle you also to their honor and respect. Even in the time of my enlistment in the executive service, how much I can recall connected with your glory. Year after year the soft heart of June, with more than Raleigh's chivalrous courtesy, has thrown her mantle of sunshine under your feet, although to-day, weeping for very joy, she bedewed it later with her laughing tears. There has at times been a little mud in the streets, — not too much, but just enough, — to prove the steadiness of your foothold. Horton, Hale, Collyer, Bolles — priests of lofty faith and inspiring eloquence — have taught you, from the sacred desk of ancient Hollis, your obligations to your fellow men and your duty to God. From this platform you have heard the rarely graceful declamation of Governor Rice, and the scholarly periods of Mayor Prince. Here to-day you see again that venerable comrade of your own, Marshall P. Wilder, twice your Commander, whose head and heart are crowned with the golden harvest of more than fourscore years. And, in my time, what a succession of commanders — gallantly representing the citizen soldier — have you not had in the commanding presences of General Martin, Colonel Wilder, Major Stevens, and Captain Cundy. You may encase, to be opened one hundred years hence, the cold letter which writes the civilization and the institutions of our time;

but you cannot send down to posterity those currents of
the blood, that speaking of the face, those generous sympathies of the heart, that common enthusiasm for the
bettering of the world, which characterize the men, whom
in the various departments of life you, to an extent, represent, and who to-day make Boston, of course, the centre
of the universe, and Massachusetts the paradise of com-
monwealths. If she be, as your toast says, " foremost
among the sisterhood of States," it is not because of the
fertility of her soil or the felicity of her situation. It is,
as the eloquent preacher said this morning, because of the
manhood of her citizens, the freedom of her thought, the
liberality of her institutions, the high standard of her
character, education, and public sentiment, and the equality of the rights of her people. There never was so glorious a democracy before. I join in your prayer : " Long
may her ascendency continue unimpaired." Not an ascendency of wealth or power for its own sake ; not an
ascendency of pride or presumption ; but an ascendency
of the civilization and happiness of all her people ; an
ascendency of good government, and of the wholesome
social life of a self-respecting and self-supporting citizenship ; an ascendency of pure homes and of honest industry, graced and enlarged with the refinements of literature, the charms of eloquence, the songs of poets, the
preaching of wholesome doctrine, and the progress of
science. At the suggestion of such a range, what names
spring to the mind ! Names not of the dead, but of those
immortal ones who live forever in the thrilling heart-beats
of Massachusetts. May this ancient and honorable company, for many years to come, minister and contribute to
the same lofty standard — to the ideal soldier's fine sense
of honor — to the true citizen's high sense of duty !

WELCOME

To the American Association for the Advancement of Science, at the Institute of Technology, August 25, 1880.

In behalf of the Commonwealth of Massachusetts, I am happy to extend cordial welcome to the American Association for the Advancement of Science. It was organized thirty-three years ago, in this her capital city, and it holds the charter of its corporate life under the act of her legislature. It has enrolled upon its membership the names of sons of hers who, by their contributions to the store of useful knowledge, have paid her the best return for the education she gave them. Among its presidents it reckons names precious in her estimation and memory, — the names of Agassiz, Peirce, Gould, and Gray. Massachusetts regards the true advancement of science with no jealous or distrustful eye, but rather as a synonym for the greater happiness of the people, the better mastery of nature, the foundation of a surer faith in God the Creator, the nearer equality of a democratic state. She rejoices in its achievements, not only when she welcomes from all the states of the Union such an illustrious gathering of scientific men as are here to-day in its interest; but also when she hears the ring of its hammer, the click of its chisel in the hands of her own artisans and mechanics, who in the varied useful and homely industries of civilization, in her machine-shops, at the wheels of her railroad cars, in her manufactories, are dignifying and elevating the lot of labor and the craft of handiwork, and

at the same time contributing to the enlargement of the
comforts, the opportunities, the usefulness of human life,
and the common weal of her citizens. For science has
no favorites in the beneficence of its results. It discloses
no secret that is not echoed around the globe. If it electrify the wire with messages of joy or of appeal, it is for
the ear of the humblest laborer as well as for that of a
king. If Bigelow invent or perfect his loom, it is that
the floor of the farmer's cottage may be carpeted as softly
to the farmer's foot, and as tastefully to his eye, as if he
were a merchant prince. Whether it be the inventions
that have developed the exhaustless power of steam; that
have made the lightning a handmaiden; that have ren-
dered warmth and light cheap and common comforts for
all alike; that have bettered our food; that have provided
transportation with marvelous economy and speed, or that
have enabled the remotest provincial to be a cosmopolite,
and have laid the world under contribution to the American citizen, high or low, rich or poor, science has taken
no exclusive as well as no backward step. Her march is
like that of the sun. Eternal dawn and brightening go
before her. The darkness flies, the shadows disappear,
and her blessing falls on all the world alike. It is in this
spirit that Massachusetts welcomes you who make science
your mistress, and who minister to her advancement. If
there be within our commonwealth populous and busy
cities and towns, alive with thrift and industry, singing
the song of the wheel, the hammer, and the loom, and
sweet with homes; if there be institutions of learning; if
there be provision broadcast for the education and elevation of all her children, independent of race or color or
condition, it is because the advancement of science has
made all this possible and easy. From Franklin and

Rumford to Morse and Bell, Massachusetts has welcomed and fostered every new addition to scientific enterprise and achievement. And yet she pays you the highest compliment by asking for yet more. Her farms, her factories, her homes, all clamor for still swifter means of development and product and comfort. If she points with pride to her great names in the realm of scientific research and progress, she also points to them still more impressively as examples of what yet greater things this generation may do for the advancement of science and the bettering of human life.

ADDRESS

At the Laying of the Corner-Stone of the Massachusetts Charitable Mechanics' Association Building on Huntington Avenue, Boston, March 15, 1881.

I BRING with pleasure to this occasion the good wishes of the Commonwealth. Your society bears her name. It was incorporated by her enactment. It is but a little younger than herself. Among its members and orators it numbers many of her magistrates and chosen ones. I cannot help referring to one of them, whose name I bear and of whose kin I am, — Governor John Davis, — as also to Hon. Marshall P. Wilder, triple promoter of agriculture, commerce, and mechanics, who is fortunately spared to grace this platform with his venerable and noble presence. Not only does your society bear the name of the Commonwealth, but it associates with her name those other titles which mark the culmination of modern civilization and suggest the crowning glories of her own progress, the dignity and beneficence of mechanical skill and labor, the blessedness of charity, the equality, the helpfulness, the magnificent power of association. It is, indeed, a significant name — the Massachusetts Charitable Mechanics' Association. While not alone, indeed, of your society, yet of it with rare fitness it may be said that its history and its work are typical of the history and the work of the Commonwealth herself. Like all her interests, it has grown beyond its own limits and lifted every other department of industry and education along with itself. Like her it has grown in purse, in power, in scope. Like her it has, in the very unfolding of its own good purposes, risen above consiaerations of profit, of benefit to an exclusive class and to limited interests, and has aimed at the welfare of a state, at the diffusion of that practical scientific knowledge and mechanical appliance which make the homes of a whole people happier and brighter, and especially at the development of manhood and character throughout all the ranks of industrial labor.

I know no words that fitly speak the debt which Massachusetts owes to the voluntary contributions and efforts of her children in these numberless lines of good works, — of charity, religion, enterprise, and of associated capital, and skill, and labor, and sentiment even, which, more than her magistrates, her laws, and her police, constitute the government of her people, and are her security and impulse. Touch such a society anywhere in its ordinary work and meetings, or at its splendid exhibitions, and lo! it is only the Massachusetts idea — the school, the church, the militia, the town - meeting — education; the higher life; the weak protected by the strong; equal rights!

Even such, to-day, in laying the corner-stone of your new and magnificent exposition building, are still the breadth and generosity of your outlook. How marvelous it is! Was it a dream or some fairy tale, — the massing of the clouds, as we have seen them at sunset, — the solid land rising from the sea, and graceful towers and palaces of gold and precious stones taking shape and shining afar, brilliant as the gorgeous hangings of the sun at close of day, and, alas! vanishing as quickly? But no dream or fairy tale is here. After years of homely, honest toil and saving, the sea has indeed been filled up, and where the tide once ebbed and flowed is now the solid land, bearing on its ample back the homes, the shops, the schoolhouses, the churches of a great city. To these you add your own splendid and spacious temple. If it were for you, if it were for your association, even if it were for the great industries you represent, and for these alone, it were hardly worth while that you should honor the laying of its foundations. But it is for the commonwealth, which means for all the world, for the bettering of all human conditions, for the enlargement of all human enjoyment and knowledge. Eloquence will lend a silver echo, and music its sweeter tones to its walls. Art will hang them with pictures. Great engines will lift their giant arms to its roof in mute and absolute obedience to man's mastery of force, and so teach the might and immortality of mind. Great themes of state will gather within its doors the concourse of the people. Schools of design will adorn it with their tracings and figures. Its exhibitions will illustrate the limitless ingenuity of human skill, and the limitless invention of human thought. It will teach, it will refine, it will inspire, it will associate, it will tie closer the common bonds of human sympathy, dependence, and progress. And year by year its record will show that through the development of industrial mechanics, based on associated action and directed in the spirit of the largest charity, all men alike, whatever their fortune or circumstances, are getting more and more of the good things of this world, — alike the finer and more comfortable raiment, alike the better food, alike the newspaper and the book, alike the luscious fruit of foreign zones, alike the blessedness of light by night and heat by day, alike the opportunity and power to grow, alike the alleviations and labor-saving helps of science ; alike for all, the comforts and betterments of a larger and nobler life !

So may it be till civilization shall reach that degree of perfection at which, with every hand and brain usefully employed, with the spirit of mutual helpfulness everywhere abroad, and with all forces combined for the common good, the whole commonwealth shall be only one great Massachusetts Charitable Mechanic Association. Erect your building in that spirit, and dedicate it to the Infinite Mind, from whom cometh that inspiration that makes man thus master of his necessities by making him the master of the world, and you will have set up in this city, amid these sacred spires that mark the houses of God, yet another temple to His praise grander in its simplicity of usefulness than Greek or Gothic ! And upon its altars shall be offered up to Him, not the smoking sacrifice of the blood of bullock or goat, but the intelligent industries, the touching suggestions of home, the beneficent helps, the myriad evidences of the unbounded progress and charity of His children.

ADDRESS

AT THE OPENING OF THE NEW ENGLAND MANUFACTURERS' AND
MECHANICS' INSTITUTE FAIR, BOSTON, AUGUST 18, 1881.

THE comprehensive speech that befits the inauguration
of this interesting exhibition of the manufacturing and
mechanical industries of New England, will be spoken by
other and more eloquent lips than my own. Mine is
rather the formal duty, in the name of the Commonwealth
which I represent, and in whose capital city this exhibition is now to be held, to proclaim its opening, to thank
the public-spirited men who have promoted it so gener-
ously, and to welcome to it the distinguished Governors of
the other New England States; the various guests who
have been bidden to this feast of labor; the representative
merchants, manufacturers, and mechanics, whose interests
centre here; the industrial classes, the product of whose
skill makes this great hall richer than a palace of the
Montezumas though groaning under heaps of gold; and,
in fine, the whole body of the people, whose civilization,
whose wealth, whose happiness, and whose homes are all
typed in this magnificent display of utility and beauty.
Yet, wonderful as are its extensiveness and variety to the
eye — suggestive as it is of material wealth; of the hum
of countless spindles; of the rush of hundreds of mountain streams; of the mute, resistless force of a thousand
giants of steamy vapor more marvelous than those of
the Arabian tale; of the freighting by land and sea of
myriad cargoes of raw material; and also of clustering

villages of factories and shops, in which that material is fashioned into food or clothing or shelter or decoration, and through which the great wealth of wages is distributed into home and church and school and into the interests and relaxations of common social life — suggestive as it is of all this material activity, it suggests yet far more the spirit that animates it all, the eternal spring of human genius that thus expands outward and upward to master the very globe, and the immortality of the growth of mind.

Two hundred and thirty-eight years ago the colonies of New England met in this Boston town to form a union for defense and common protection. Here to-day they meet again, in the persons of their Governors and representative men of business, fearful no more of neighboring or foreign foe, eager not to avert by common array the perils of invading war, but to stimulate by common enterprise the industries and arts of peace. Fellow citizens of New England, those are *our* Olympic games. Here we rub out, if any vestige of it indeed be left, the churlishness of the provincialism of boundary lines. Here we learn that there is no political state, except the common prosperity and happiness of all. Here we cultivate that patriotism which means the common good. Here we find that our interests are all woven into one; and that, as commerce thrives, as manufacture plies its skillful hand, as labor is employed, as capital casts its bread upon the waters to find it after many days, so year by year with accelerating swiftness come accumulating upon our country, and upon all it bears or adopts, a finer life, new resources for body and mind, a literature wider spread, the works of science and philosophy in the shepherd's hands, the canal-boy's dream realized in a throne founded upon the suffrages and in the hearts of a free people. Yes, these are our Olympic games; but the races we run are of the head and not of the feet; the wrestling-matches are not of human sinews, but of the forces of nature grappling, under the direction of human skill, with the fibres of the field, with the inertia of ores, with wood and stone, not to fling them to the earth, but to raise and train them into a million hand-servants of usefulness and luxury; and the prize is not a fading olive wreath, but that perfection of blessings, that dream of all other lands and lots, — a New England home.

In the cause, therefore, of a common advancing material prosperity, and yet even more in the cause of patriotism, of education, of a community of the highest interests, and of the intellectual and moral good of the people, I welcome you all to this New England Manufacturers' and Mechanics' Institute. I trust it will inure to an increased activity and development of our manufacturing and mechanical interests; that it will stimulate enterprise, production, and the investment of capital here at home; that it will aid to preserve and also to increase the supremacy of New England in the field of skilled labor and industrial and fine art; and that, because of it, our watercourses will turn new wheels; our deserted farms bloom afresh; our hillside villages spring to new life; our young men and women look not abroad for employment; the magnificent industrial capacities of Maine and New Hampshire find their fulfillment; the verdure of the Vermont mountains reflect yet richer farms; the industries of Rhode Island and Connecticut advance even upon their already marvelous thrift. I am sure it will tend to instruct the public mind, to refine the public taste, to lighten for all the drudgery of toil, to encourage the decoration of homes, and to mould to finer touches the art of the people's living.

And now for the more comprehensive word that befits this inauguration day of the exhibition. It should come from one whose information grasps the material interests, not only of New England but of the Union; who is familiar not only with manufactures and mechanics but with commerce and trade, and whose researches extend also to that older and nobler science, the reverent culture of the soil itself. It would be well, too, we think, that he should be one who, holding some national charge allied to all these pursuits, can speak the broad and unsectional word, which embraces the welfare of the whole American people, and welds their sympathies as well as their interests closer together. If to these qualities we can add the orator's voice and port, his elegance of declamation, and his copious thought and power of illustration, we shall lack nothing. And nothing certainly do we lack; for I now have the pleasure of presenting to you the fitly-chosen speaker of the day — the Hon. George B. Loring, Commissioner of Agriculture of the United States.

WELCOME

I AM grateful for the courtesy which accords to me the pleasure of sincerely though briefly welcoming the National Conference of Charities to Massachusetts. Especially so far as its delegates come from outside her own borders and represent other jurisdictions, our Commonwealth is glad of an opportunity to greet them, to exhibit to them her public institutions, and to receive instruction from them in the science of charity and correction. You have met together in Boston, her political, social, and commercial capital. This is her State House, in which sat Andrew, Horace Mann, and Dr. Howe, — names forever associated with those causes of humanity, education, and charity in which you are engaged, and to which she has never been disloyal. As you entered the hall below, you saw the battle-flags of her regiments, there sacredly preserved as mementoes, not so much of fraternal strife as of that healthier, freer, and nobler union, in behalf of which they were borne by her sons to victory. The chamber in which you sit is that in which the popular branch of her General Court meets less to make laws than to hear all causes of grievance, reform, and progress, and especially to promote the general advance of that science to which you give specific study. I should misrepresent her if in any trite commonplaces of provincial pride I boasted of her correctional and charitable institutions, to the inspection

of which she cordially invites your criticism 'and suggestion quite as much as your praise, except perhaps in this,
that they are absolutely exempt from political entangle-
ment.   For at least to this height she has attained, that in
all this matter she values her edifices and appointments,
her officers and managers as nothing compared with the
best care and true welfare of those dependents, afflicted
by ills of body or of mind, or even by crime, who are her
wards.   And to this also, that she recognizes any gain she
may have made in the science of charity and correction as
only elementary, and but the threshold of the future, and
so will thank you for any inspiration or enlightenment
that will help her onward.   And yet, how great a gain it
has been, and what satisfaction it affords and justifies,
when she compares the present with the past, — the separate prison for women, a very asylum and house of refor-
mation ; the state prison with its greatly increased population, yet its at once lighter and more perfect discipline,
and its riddance of nearly all the old varieties of degrading punishments ; the state primary school, a healthy and
happy avenue through which the little pauper children of
the state go speedily forth to homes ; the more humane and
less restraining treatment of the insane ; the education
even of the idiot; the giving of ears to the deaf, a tongue
to the dumb, and sight to the blind ! Nor let me, in inviting your attention to the charities of Massachusetts,
fail to assure you how much of whatever good has resulted from them is due to private enterprise and contribution ; how much has been accomplished by the forceful
and telling unity of purpose and action, which has come
from the consolidation of these private and local benefi-
cences into county organizations, auxiliary boards, and
what in Boston is termed the Associated Charities ; and

especially how in our Commonwealth the women have come to the front, not only with their sympathies, which are always alive, but with the brightest business tact and administrative ability.

The causes in behalf of which you meet appeal so touchingly to the best sentiments of the human heart, that these spring to the lips for utterance at the very thought of your coming together — at the very sight of so much intelligence and human kindness converging from all quarters of the land, representing its centres of need and of public spirit, and gathering to deliberate upon still better methods by which to relieve misery, to cure infirmities, to stimulate self - respect and self - support. And yet, fortunately for the poor, the insane, the criminal, you meet as a matter, not of sentiment, but of science and practical and economic work. That certainly is the true charity, most just alike to the state and to the beneficiary, which puts him above the patronage and emasculation of alms, and in the way of self-support. That is the true correction which brings home to the criminal the conviction that the wages of honest labor are better than the wages of sin. The problem is easy to state, but almost too intricate to solve, for the field on which you enter is as illimitable as the needs and frailties of humanity. Your work is one which is never accomplished, which is always expanding, and the success of which is never found in any resting-places of final results, but in the constancy of new demands and further progress. With the increase of immigration, the rapid growth of cities, the tumorous excrescences alike of wealth and poverty, and the inroads of ignorance into even the older and more advanced states, the problem is never solved, its intricacies only shift. In welcoming you, therefore, let me also in the name of the Commonwealth, and of her unfortunate, her poor and infirm in mind and body, to whose bettering your session will be devoted, thank you for what you have done and are doing. The state must always needs move slowly, and your inquiries and observations are the best forerunner of its legislation. The myriad fingers of private benevolence and activity meet the necessities which spring like weeds, yet lose half their value if not directed by the best intelligence and coöperation. What is impulse and misdirection, it is yours to organize into steady principles and forces. To you we look for fresh methods of staying pauperism, so that we shall not have it to maintain; of preventing intemperance, so that we shall not have its intolerable and degrading burden to bear; of reforming the criminal, so that we shall not have him to punish. And for your part in all this perpetually recurring, yet always advancing work, I only represent the gratitude of the people when I thank you and wish for you in this conference and all your endeavors successful and illuminating progress. It is for me not to make any specific observations, but only to extend to you this general word of greeting. You have come to Massachusetts at the time of her summer glory. Those of you who come from the interior of the country will miss the boundlessness of your prairies and wheat-fields; but you will find the cool shadows of woods and hills, and will taste the fresh and salty breath of the sea. And be assured, to whatever she has, whether of natural beauty, of historical associations, or of social science, Massachusetts cordially welcomes you, alike for your own sake and for that of the enlightened and public-spirited constituencies you represent, and especially because you are of those of whom it has been said, Blessed is he that considereth the poor.

RESPONSE

For the Commonwealth at the Centennial Dinner of the Massachusetts Medical Society, Music Hall, Boston, June 8, 1881.

I am sure, Mr. President and members of the Massachusetts Medical Society, that one of the fundamental though unwritten laws of the Commonwealth is a sound mind in a sound body. A hundred years ago last October she provided for the former by adopting the constitution under which her institutions of piety, education, and progress have thriven from that day to this; and a year later, and nearly a hundred years ago, in order to promote the latter she incorporated the Massachusetts Medical Society over the broad sign manual of her first governor, and put the lives and limbs of her citizens into its perilous keeping. I say perilous not altogether lightly, recalling the reference you have just made, sir, to a "century of medicine," the very thought of which almost necessitates the attendance of a physician. And besides, you celebrate to-day a centennial not more of original beneficence than of constant progress out of error and ignorance into truth and knowledge. Of all the professions, that of medicine, I take it, is the most experimental and tentative, — a consideration, by the way, which is very delightful for the scientist, but of somewhat doubtful comfort to the patient, in spite of the remark which Dr. Williams has just made, that its operations are performed so "quickly, safely, and pleasantly." During the century the common law has scarce taken a step. The pulpit has but amplified, not always successfully, the Sermon on the Mount. But without knowing anything about it — may it be long before I do know anything about it — I gather that medicine has made its splendid advance by forgetting and discarding its yesterdays. Of all the sciences, this, then, should be, as it is, a liberal science; and, while it gains so powerfully from such an organization as yours, it will take care to escape the one danger that attends all organizations, — the danger of limitation, — a danger which, however, in the broadening light of day, ought to cause little apprehension.

The Commonwealth, therefore, cordially responds with good wishes for the health and long life of this, which is one of its oldest and most beneficent incorporations. As your toast suggests, medicine and politics go well together, though in each case I doubt not it is much pleasanter to administer than to take the dose. There is certainly no better or more adroit politician than the doctor. And both medicine and politics are learning in the art of cure — one that it is better to recognize nature, let her have her head, not irritate her, but keep her well fed and in the line of her own direction; the other that it is better and just as easy to recognize not the worst but the best sentiment of the people and let them alone as far as possible, only seeing to it that they have a fair chance, good training and education, equal rights, and, of all things else, pure air, pure water, and, especially within ten miles of Boston, good drainage. If medicine gave the name of Warren to Massachusetts, she in turn gave it to the country and to history, and has forever engraved it on the loftier heights; and she rejoices that after the lapse of a hundred years it is still one of the most promising upon her roll.   Nor did Warren more patriotically devote his life to the cause of patriotism than your own associates gave theirs from 1861 to 1865, who were in every command of the war, and on whom its horrors and ghastly spectacles fell all unrelieved.   But your chief significance, after all, to the great body of the people of the Commonwealth, all of whom and not a part of whom I represent, is not immediately in your scientific progress, splendid as it has been, not so much in your patriotic and political services, great as those have been, but in your relation to their homes.   In them, in the relief of pain, in the sympathy of attendance, in the emancipation of wife and child from sickness and death, in the tenderness and confidence of the friendship of the family doctor, you have your warmest hold upon their gratitude and affection.   It is not for me to enlarge upon your broader spheres of work, or the reliance placed on your judgment in the supervision and administration of the hospital, the board of public health, the fight with contagion and epidemic, and the great hygienic preventions and safeguards.   The Commonwealth appreciates it all.   She recognizes what a century it has been of beneficent, scientific, devoted progress, to which my lips, inexpert in its mysteries, can only pay the tribute of mute but open admiration.   You may have been impatient with her sometimes.   She may not humor your every project.   She may depart from your advice now and then in the legislative construction of a board, or in refusing to apply to your branch of American industry the doctrine of protection; but, taken by and large, her public sentiment gives you your due, vindicates her honesty of purpose and in the main her soundness of judgment; and she will stand by you for another hundred years to come, as she has stood by you in the hundred years gone by, in all generous, onward steps, so many of which you have already taken, and so many more of which you will hereafter take, in the work of saving the bodies, and, so far, of saving the souls, of her children.

RESPONSE

AT THE BANQUET AT UNION HALL, CAMBRIDGE, MASS., ON THE
TWO HUNDRED AND FIFTIETH ANNIVERSARY OF ITS SETTLE-
MENT, DECEMBER 28, 1880.

THE conviction has been growing upon my mind of
late, Mr. Mayor, that somehow or other the times are out
of joint. Either my friends were indeed right when they
said that I was too young for public place, — though I
never heard that objection raised against my worthy pre-
decessor, John Winthrop, who was of the same age when
he became governor, — or else everything and everybody
have suddenly become unaccountably old. When the
orator of the day told of the little boy, who, questioning
him about the recent civil war in which he bore so illustrious a part, asked him if he was at the battle of Bunker
Hill, it did not surprise me. My only wonder is that he
did not suspect Colonel Higginson of having been in the
Pequot War, or even of being the redoubtable Miles
Standish himself. Hardly an event has there been during
the short term of my administration that was not from
an hundred to two hundred and fifty years old ; and last
week, at Plymouth, the occasion ran even ten years beyond that. If the thing goes much farther, I shall feel
like wearing silver buckles and a ruffle, and putting iron
pots on the heads of my staff, which would add little to
the thickness of their skulls, but much to the improvement of their personal appearance. How delightful it
would be, and how refreshing, if for a moment we could

only turn from the past, and, looking into the future, celebrate in advance the five hundredth anniversary of the incorporation of Cottage City, or the violent annexation of the best part of Belmont to the city of Cambridge! It would give us such an admirable opportunity, which we should certainly improve, of dwelling upon our own services, our sacrifices, our virtues, which I dare say are grander than any which have gone before, and upon the simplicity and excellence of our magistrates, the dignity of our mayors and executive councilors, the stern but salutary government of our colleges, the quiet demeanor of our boys, and the repressed and sombre lives of our young women. How charming it would be to mouse out the musty manuscript of the oration of one Colonel Higginson, veteran of a great war and then in the militia service of Massachusetts, and whose quaint conceits and honest boasts of the civilization of his day would certainly be pardonable in one who had only the education and advantages of the nineteenth century, but whose pure, though antiquated, eloquence would go far to show that there were giants also in those days! I am not certain that, had our ancestors anticipated these anniversaries, they would not have most carefully concealed the dates of these early settlements, and so have spared their descendants the infliction of being compelled to hear, and, what is infinitely sadder, my friends, being compelled to speak, these conventional anniversary addresses.

But seriously, Mr. Mayor, having been present at many similar occasions, I can most truly say here, what I have most truly said at all the rest of them, that nowhere is there such a wealth of historic interest; nowhere such a succession of significant events; nowhere such elements of high, sterling character; nowhere such enterprise, faith, courage, devotion ; nowhere such love and appreciation of learning, and such contribution to its diffusion, as in the early history of the time and place which you now cele-brate. Comprehensive and conciliatory as that statement is, it is yet the simple truth. Each of these anniversaries we do well to celebrate by oration and banquet, by peal of bells and roar of cannon, by the presence of citizen men and women, by strains of music and decorations of halls, and by the spirited songs of children who bring their impressible minds to have photographed upon them the glory and goodness of the past. For each of them is a type of all the rest, and all pay common tribute to a common origin, a common ancestry, and a common train-ing, to which we are all alike indebted. If there is a con-tinual glitter through the whole year, it is because, all around her coronet, Massachusetts is studded thick with jewels.

With you it may well be your pride that it is light and honor and growth all the way down in one broadening path, from the beginning till this day. When your orator rose this afternoon it seemed to me his only burden was his embarrassment of riches. How well he bore that bur-den those who were present and listened to him can bear witness. Winthrop and Dudley were in at your birth. The sacred name of the apostle John Eliot, still worthily honored, is associated with the history of a portion of your ancient town. With Cambridge is hallowed in every heart and every memory the establishment of that little college, which has now become, in this your city, the most famous university in America. And where learn-ing is, there religion, patriotism, and poetry also take root. From here Hooker went to found a pious city. Upon these greens the American army was drawn up.

Under these elms Washington drew his sword and took command. Along these highways marched Putnam, Stark, Green, and those other heroes, at the bare mention of whose names — so tender is always the Revolutionary memory — the heart stirs to patriotic tears quite as much as it stirs with patriotic pride. On your shores landed that flaunting detachment of British soldiers, which, after their memorable march to Lexington and Concord, came back with broken ranks and trailing colors. Here is the house of Lowell; this is the birthplace of Holmes, whose wit and song and story and talk are that very health, the promotion of which has been his humbler and every-day calling. And here lives Longfellow, to apply to whom any descriptive praise except to call him poet is to show what is the poverty on my tongue of that language which in his moulding is only the potter's clay of grace and beauty and tenderness. Here, too, was the volunteering — history again repeating itself — of your best blood and bravest patriotism in the last great fight for liberty and union.

But it is not for me to attempt an enumeration of names and events which could only be an injustice by reason of its meagreness. Nor may I refer to my own memories of Cambridge; or to my first sight of its towers, one morning in June, so near the dawn that even the "hourlies" were not yet up and running, when at fourteen years of age, going to my college entrance examination, I walked all the way from Boston, keeping the right-hand side of Main Street, every inch of which is blistered into my memory to this day; or to the later hour when I sat crying in utter homesickness on the western steps of Gore Hall. That was certainly two hundred and fifty years ago, and the hearts that throbbed most at such a poor matter as my boyish heart-break are long since at rest.

I said a broadening path of growth. That is true. Venerable and honorable as is the past, our faces should be set toward the future. It is to the future that Massachusetts, always alert and progressive, points her finger. If she reveres and honors the time gone by, as you revere and honor it to-day, it is only that she may be stimulated to better work in the time to come. We would not go back if we could. To do so would be to sleep like Rip Van Winkle, and wake to find that the world had swept by us, and out of sight, our garments out at elbow and our muskets crumbling. We may not have improved much, as we certainly have not, upon the purpose, the spirit, the moral force, the ultimate aim for self and for those who were to come after, which distinguished our fathers ; but the expression, the appointments, the methods, are a thousand times better. Religion is still the same, but its garment of doctrine and formula has been renewed more than once. Character is still the man ; but education, which is his fingers and his safeguard, has extended till it commands every spring and force of nature, and every avenue of intelligence and science. Our food is better, our clothing is better, our health is better, our books, our homes, our enjoyments are all better. Our children are healthier, and life is more worth living to-day than it was then. Let us, however, not forget that if it is so it is because the germ was in the early soil, and because our fathers, who planted it and nurtured it, were true to themselves and true to us. Therefore let us honor their memories, and let us hand down to those who shall come after us the opportunity and the purpose for a gain and a growth greater than our own. There is one word that sums it all, and that word is progress ; that word is Massachusetts ; that word is every human soul, every home, every town within her borders ; that word, emphatically, is this your beautiful and classic, your ancient and famous city of Cambridge, this graceful cluster of homes upon the banks of the Charles, this sparkling gem upon the fair forehead of the Commonwealth.

RESPONSE

AT THE DINNER OF THE OXFORD BEARS, AT GILBERT'S HALL, PORTLAND, MAINE, MAY 27, 1885.

I CONFESS, Mr. Chairman, that too often called, as I am, to these festival occasions, yet I was downright glad to get an invitation to this one. If there was ever a thorough-going provincial, if there was ever a native of the fields that was loyal to rural life, if ever a bear went out of rugged Oxford County that never lost his sweet tooth for her honey, I claim to share in that distinction. Did not, Mr. Emery, your father and mine interchange their rhyming muses over the hills of Paris and Buckfield? Was I not born in one of Oxford's nestling cradles, in a village lovelier than sweet Auburn, loveliest village of the plain, — in a happier valley than the Abyssinian seclusion of Rasselas, — by the side of one of Oxford's streams, whose music sang me, a child, to sleep, and has sung in my dreams ever since, — under the exquisite elms that are the grace of her landscape, — and among the fairest hills that ever broke the golden sunsets of the west or lifted the luxuriant foliage of a Maine summer? Did not " old Streaked " teach my youth the glory of the mountains as well as feed me with the nutritious and wholesome blue-berry? Did I not graduate at Hebron Academy, and do I not recall that temple of learning as the most imposing architectural pile and spire that ever awed a schoolboy? Was it not there I stammered my first declamation, and in a very still, small voice thundered Cicero's question to

Catiline, demanding how long he proposed to abuse our
patience? Was it not at Hebron that the song of the
frogs and the glow of the fire-fly associated themselves
forever in the mind of a homesick lad with a tender mel-
ancholy which to this day they never fail to revive, little
as you would suspect it from my personal appearance?
Was it not of his poverty-stricken term at Hebron that
my father wrote to me, referring to his own struggles in
lines which I recall: —

> " How I was poor and lame and lean,
>   Wore homespun clothes of bottle green ;
>   Your grandsire's wedding coat resigned,
>   Turned inside out and patched behind ;
>   My brother Tom's old vest of blue
>   Five summers after it was new.
>   And how I traveled to recite
>   Two miles at morning, two at night,
>   Because I could not then afford
>   To pay the price of nearer board,
>   Or people nearer did not choose
>   To take their pay in making shoes."

Why, sir, Oxford County to me is a volume of poems,
a paradise of nature. Her crests of blue against the
summer sky, and in winter white with glistening snow,
her pure waters, her cool woods, her picturesque roads
winding over hill and down dale, her exquisite intermin-
gling of forest and farm, are such a natural park of loveliness and magnificence as no metropolitan wealth or art
can ever imitate.

For one, I owe it a deeper debt. Enlarging and edu-
cating as were its physical influences, I pay my tribute
still more gratefully to the living influences of its people.
In American life and struggle, I believe there is no such
education as that of a country boy's contact in school and

at all times with the social democracy of a country such as Oxford County typifies, — absolutely meeting the ideal of a free and equal people, and ignorant of such a thing as caste or class.

Add to such a democracy the elements of the education of the common schools, the unfettered exercise of religious freedom, the popular political discussion of the street corner, the store, and the hay-field, the frequent vacancies of leisure, the common knowledge of men and things, the splendid ingrained inheritance of English common law ripened into the maxims, habits, converse, and system of the people, the absence on the one hand of great accumulations of wealth, and on the other of any consciousness of the deprivations of extreme poverty, and especially that unconscious unreserve and inartificiality of intercourse which made the hewer of stone the free and easy, if not superior, disputant as well as companion of the owner of the field, — add all these, and you have an atmosphere of education, out of which no boy could emerge and not have a fitting for future life such as the metropolis with its schools, the university with its colleges, could not give, a homely familiarity with the popular mind, an inbred sympathy with the masses, not artificial or assumed, but a part of character itself, and a helpful agency in public service and in useful conduct in life. Its fruits you see to-day, and for years have seen, in the elements which from rural counties like Oxford have gone into the busy avenues of our national life and given enterprise, growth, success to the business, the government, the literature, and the progress of our country.

Yes, my friends, I believe we are here to utter our gratitude to the men and women who gave a popular tone to Oxford County worthy of her hills and the grandeur and strength of her physical magnificence. My gratitude is from a full heart. I recognize with profound emotion the resolute, generous, and fruitful purpose and force which our fathers put into their farms and water-courses and trading-posts. I look back and behold worth and highmindedness driving the oxen afield, cutting the wood, tending the sawmill, leading the training field and the election, doing neighborly turns and kindnesses, bartering the worsted mitten over the counter, and making the wholesomest texture of a pastoral, provincial life the world has ever seen or ever will see, — the ideal combination of industry, equality, freedom, intelligence, and high character. We talk nowadays of poverty; we pity our city full of poor; we create and foster our associated charities. And yet you have among you in this great city hardly a family so scanty in their means, so comfortless in their homes, — thanks to the inventions, improvements, and distributions of modern times, — as the pioneers of Oxford County less than a hundred years ago. We little realize the rapid spread of those means of making life easier, which of later years have given to the poorest hearth comforts which then the richest did not dream of. It was the best blood of Massachusetts — pure English stock, little changed even to this day, the best families of Pilgrim and Puritan descent — which after the Revolutionary war made their way to Oxford County. But like all pioneers, they had little of this world's goods, and brought little except their splendid inheritance of worth and character, their brave hearts and honest, hardworking hands. How illustrative of all this straitened circumstance is the story of that half fisherman and half shoemaker, pestered by debt, and at last selling his little farm in the mother commonwealth, and with his wife and brood of children, his kit of tools and scanty household furniture, sailing by packet from Plymouth to Salem, and thence journeying overland in a pioneer's wagon, which held all he had, a hundred and fifty miles into the uplands of Oxford County, Maine, in 1806. How often my father, God bless him, has told me of their arrival at the foot of the mile-long hill, at the top of which was the journey's end, with its half-finished house and half-cleared farm; of himself, six years old, and his older brother, running barefoot ahead of the team to get the first glimpse of their future home, — a cheerless enclosure of boards, but to them a paradise, — stopping now and then to pick the thistles from their hardy little feet. There is a famous picture painted by a French artist called the First Arrival. It represents a lofty cliff overlooking a landscape of the richest luxuriance, and itself affluent with vines and sunshine. On it are the crumbling walls of an ancient castle that even in its ruins suggests the pomp and circumstance of wealth and power. A gay party of youths and maidens have clambered up to look at it and from it. Foremost, the first to arrive is a beautiful girl, richly dressed, herself a flushed dream of loveliness, a child of opulence and luxury, who for one bright summer morning spices the ennui of satiety with a fresh touch of nature and the pure breath of the mountain air. It is a rare picture, and yet I wish some artist might draw, as I in imagination can see, that poor, ragged, barefooted boy who had never a luxury of food or clothing or amusement, whose bare feet were pricked with thistles, who climbed that Oxford hill, and who, though he looked not on baronial castles or landscapes luxuriant with vines, yet thrilled with a New England boy's pride in his father's freehold, and with a New England boy's prophetic unconsciousness, if I may so say, of a chance and a future

for him also in the world, as well as for the most favored
child of fortune — for him a Latin grammar, though a bor-
rowed one; for him an entrance into the academy, though
but for a single term ; for him a place in the community and
a claim on its respect and honor ; and for him the means to
give his own children the opportunities of education and
learning which had been denied himself. Pardon me if I
recall this and the universal hardships of those days, —
the great families of children, the narrow means, — even
the neighborly lending and borrowing from the scanty
pork barrel, the footings knit of winter nights to buy
the comfort now and then of groceries from the village
store, the rude unfinished house round which the snow-
blast howled, the green wood drawn from the night's
snowdrift and cut and split to make the morning fire on
the open hearth, the coarse, plain, unvaried fare, the long,
hard, poorly paying journeys to distant markets, the stress
of debt, the tugging strain of years to turn the woodland
into tillage, — and yet running through all this toil and
privation and hardship an infinite cheer and humor, and
also the courage, the Pilgrim earnestness, the religious
faith, the love of family and country, the hope and sacrifice
for children, the inborn instinct of the freeholder, which
redeemed and glorified all else, and to-day command our
respect and pride as the qualities of no other ancestry
could. If it was poverty, it was not the poverty of dependence or charity or disparagement in any form, but
poverty with independence and pride, living within such
means as were its own, and finding enough even at that
with which to build the church and the academy, to
keep the law, to have the schoolmaster, to buy a book, to
get the contents of the newspaper, to understand the elements of constitutional and common law, to vote honestly

and intelligently, to go to the legislature, to discuss in town meeting the affairs of town and state and country, and to fill out the full measure of the enlightened citizen of the republic.

I do not forget that there were other and very marked shadings of the picture, but this was the sort of men who were most distinctive of Oxford County, and who gave it character. What splendid stock it was! What sturdy English names, — those Mitchells, Lincolns, Holmeses, Lorings, Emerys, Parsons, Taylors, Cushings, Halls, Bicknells, Perrys, Washburns, Hamlins, Aldens, Mortons, Whitmans, and hundreds more! Hardly a family, however hard its fight with adverse circumstances, that has not been a contributor to the enterprise, the scholarship, the statesmanship, the patriotism, that have made our country great.

In every avenue of its usefulness you find their trace. You hear their eloquence in every court and congress. You saw the flash of their swords in every battle for freedom. Well may we recall the men of Oxford with pride and gratitude. No narrow scope was theirs. They nursed the schools. They valued and exemplified and maintained the education of the people. They contended for good politics. They discussed fundamental issues. Could you awake the voices of the past you would hear them also treat of reform, of tariff and revenue, and of the relations of the general government to its local components, with all the vigor and enlightenment which we sometimes think to be the exclusive attainment of our own time.

I thank you, sir, for permitting me to join with you in your tribute to Oxford. The occasion touches me very tenderly, for it carries my heart and betrays my utterance into sacred memories of my own boyhood and home.

They come freshly back to me, as yours to you, and I stand again at the threshold of an opening world, with the sunrise on my face. Again I sit at the blessed family fireplace as of old, unthinking then of the love and fervent devotion to my welfare and advancement to which I owe everything, and which to me now, looking back, is all so clear. I knew not then that angels' wings brushed my cheeks. Now I strain my eyes to heaven to catch their flight.

ORATION

Before the Grand Army Posts of Suffolk County at Tremont Temple, Boston, May 30, 1882.

I GRATEFULLY acknowledge your courtesy, veterans and members of the Suffolk posts of the Grand Army, in inviting me, a civilian, to speak for you this day. I should shrink from the task, however, did I not know that, in this, your purpose is to honor again the Commonwealth of which I am the official representative. By recent enactment she has made the day you celebrate one of her holy days, — a day sacred to the memory of her patriot dead and to the inspiration of patriotism in her living. Henceforward, she emblazons it upon the calendar of the year with the consecrated days that have come down from the Pilgrim and the Puritan, with Christmas Day and with the birthdays of Washington and American Independence. So she commits herself afresh to the eternal foundations, which the fathers laid, of piety, education, freedom, justice, law, and love of country. The time will come indeed, and speedily, when none of you shall remain to observe it, and when the last survivor, shouldering his crutch no more, shall lie down to rest with no comrade left to shed a tear or flower upon his grave. But the service you did, the sacrifice you made, the example you taught, more immortal than your crumbling dust, will forever live and illume the world, as in the heavens, speeding so far from us that the eye sees not the vapor that enshrouds them, the stars shine only in purer and eternal glory. I can understand that, when the war closed, the same disinterested and single loyalty, which compelled the true citizen to arms, made many a soldier shrink from even the appearance of farther display, either by joining your organization or by publicly engaging in the decoration of graves. But with the lapse of time, with the inroads on the ranks, with this statutory recognition by the commonwealth, — a recognition not more apt in desert than in time, — Memorial Day will hereafter gather around it not only the love and tears and pride of the generations of the people, but more and more, in its inner circle of tenderness, the linking memories of every comrade, so long as one survives. As the dawn ushers it in, tinged already with the exquisite flush of hastening June, and sweet with the bursting fragrance of her roses, the wheels of time will each year roll back, and, lo! John Andrew is at the state house, inspiring Massachusetts with the throbbing of his own great heart; Abraham Lincoln, wise and patient and honest and tender and true, is at the nation's helm; the North is one broad blaze; the boys in blue are marching to the front; the fife and drum are on every breeze; the very air is patriotism; Phil Sheridan, forty miles away, dashes back to turn defeat to victory; Farragut, lashed to the mast-head, is steaming into Mobile Harbor; Hooker is above the clouds, — ay, now indeed forever above the clouds; Sherman marches through Georgia to the sea; Grant has throttled Lee with the grip that never lets go; Richmond falls; the armies of the republic pass in that last great review at Washington; Custer's plume is there, but Kearney's saddle is empty; and, now again, our veterans come marching home to receive the welcome of a grateful people, and to stack in Doric Hall the tattered flags which Massachusetts forever hence shall wear above her heart.

In memory of the dead, in honor of the living, for inspiration to our children, we gather to-day to deck the graves of our patriots with flowers, to pledge commonwealth and town and citizen to fresh recognition of the surviving soldier, and to picture yet again the romance, the reality, the glory, the sacrifice of his service. As if it were but yesterday, you recall him. He had but turned twenty. The exquisite tint of youthful health was in his cheek. His pure heart shone from frank, outspeaking eyes. His fair hair clustered from beneath his cap. He had pulled a stout oar in the college race, or walked the most graceful athlete on the village green. He had just entered on the vocation of his life. The doorway of his home at this season of the year was brilliant in the dewy morn with the clambering vine and fragrant flower, as in and out he went, the beloved of mother and sisters, and the ideal of a New England youth: —

> " In face and shoulders like a god he was ;
> For o'er him had the goddess breathed the charm
> Of youthful locks, the ruddy glow of youth,
> A generous gladness in his eyes : such grace
> As carver's hand to ivory gives, or when
> Silver or Parian stone in yellow gold
> Is set."

The unreckoned influences of the great discussion of human rights had insensibly moulded him into a champion of freedom. He had passed no solitary and sleepless night watching the armor which he was to wear when dubbed next day with the accolade of knighthood. But over the student's lamp or at the fireside's blaze he had passed the nobler initiate of a heart and mind trained to a fine sense of justice and to a resolution equal to the sacrifice of life itself in behalf of right and duty. He knew nothing of the web and woof of politics, but he knew instinctively the needs of his country. His ideal was Philip Sidney, not Napoleon. And when the drum beat, when the first martyr's blood sprinkled the stones of Baltimore, he took his place in the ranks and went forward. You remember his ingenuous and glowing letters to his mother, written as if his pen were dipped in his very heart. How novel seemed to him the routine of service, the life of camp and march! How eager the wish to meet the enemy and strike his first blow for the good cause! What pride at the promotion that came and put its chevron on his arm or its strap upon his shoulder! How graphically he described his sensation in the first battle, the pallor that he felt creeping up his face, the thrilling along every nerve, and then the utter fearlessness when once the charge began and his blood was up! Later on, how gratefully he wrote of the days in hospital, of the opening of the box from home, of the generous distributing of delicacies that loving ones had sent, and of the never-to-be-forgotten comfort of the gentle nurse whose eyes and hands seemed to bring to his bedside the summer freshness and health of the open windows of his and her New England homestead! No Amazon was she with callous half-breast; but her whole woman's heart was devoted, as were the hearts of all her sisters at the North, to lightening the hardships and pain of war. Let her praise never fail to mingle in the soldier's tribute, or her abilities be belittled in a land to whose salvation and honor she contributed as nobly in her service as he in his.

They took him prisoner. He wasted in Libby and grew gaunt and haggard with the horror of his sufferings and with pity for the greater horror of the sufferings of his comrades who fainted and died at his side. He saw his schoolmate panting with the fever of thirst, yet shot like a dog for reaching across the line to drink the stagnant water a dog would have scorned. He tunneled the earth and escaped. Hungry and weak, in terror of recapture, he followed by night the pathway of the railroad. Upon its timbers, hoar with frost, he tottered in the dark over rivers that flowed deep beneath his treacherous foothold. He slept in thickets and sank in swamps. In long and painful circuits he stole around hamlets where he dared not ask for shelter. He saw the glitter of horsemen who pursued him. He knew the bloodhound was on his track. A faithful negro — good Samaritan — took compassion on him, bound up his wounds, and set him on his way. He reached the line ; and, with his hand grasping at freedom, they caught and took him back to his captivity. He was exchanged at last ; and you remember, when he came home on a short furlough, how manly and war-worn he had grown. But he soon returned to the ranks and to the welcome of his comrades. They loved him for his manliness, his high bearing, his fine sense of honor. They felt the nobility of conduct and character that breathed out from him. They recall him now alike with tears and pride. In the rifle-pits around Petersburg you heard his steady voice and firm command. The bullet of the sharp-shooter picked off the soldier who stood at his side and who fell dying in his arms, one last brief message whispered and faithfully sent home. It was a forlorn hope, — the charge of the brave regiment to which he belonged, reduced now by three years' long fighting to a hundred veterans, conscious that somebody had blundered yet grimly obedient to duty. Some one who saw him then fancied that he seemed that day like one who forefelt the end. But there was no flinching as he charged. He had just turned to give a cheer when the fatal ball struck him. There was a convulsion of the upward hand. His eyes, pleading and loyal, turned their last glance to the flag. His lips parted. He fell dead, and at nightfall lay with his face to the stars. Home they brought him, fairer than Adonis over whom the goddess of beauty wept. They buried him in the village churchyard under the green turf. Year by year his comrades and his kin, nearer than comrades, scatter his grave with flowers. His picture hangs on the homestead walls. Children look up at it and ask to hear his story told. It was twenty years ago; and the face is so young, so boyish and fair, that you cannot believe he was the hero of twenty battles, a veteran in the wars, a leader of men, brave, cool, commanding, great. Do you ask who he was? He was in every regiment and every company. He went out from every Massachusetts village. He sleeps in every Massachusetts burying-ground. Recall romance, recite the names of heroes of legend and song, but there is none that is his peer. Can you think of him and not count the cost of such a precious life, not thrill with gratitude at such a sacrifice, not ask why such promise, such hope, such worth, should have been cut down? I know not why it is that, if the future is always progress, the past is always sacrifice, unless it be that in the nation as in the man sacrifice is the soil and seed of progress. I know not why it is in the providence of God that through blood — not the sacrifice of rams and goats, but the blood of human hearts — the great gains of human freedom have had their impulse, unless it be that in the laws of growth, as in the laws of light, it is the red rays that are strongest and that first shine through and flash the dawn, foretelling the pure white fire of the uprising sun. But this we do know:

that, search history through, and you shall find no more heroic record of self-sacrifice, of courage, of the flower of youth giving itself to death for right and country's sake. Massachusetts will never forget the memory of these her martyrs. Their lives are insensibly moulding the character of her children at school or by fireside even while the busy man of years and of affairs may almost seem to have forgotten them. With you she weeps over their turf and crowns them with the laurel wreath.

Yes, why was it? Why do we recall all this? Because the sacrifice is lost in the consummation, death is swallowed up in victory; because it was not a nipped bud but the full flower, not a life cut off, but a life rounded and complete; because the high ideals, the lofty purposes, the forward-looking ambition to be of service in the world were all fulfilled, not defeated, in these young men. If in our pride of conquest, if in these organizations and festivals our purpose were simply to count our excess of victories, to glory in superiority of endurance, strength, and numbers, to echo the gladiator's roar of triumph, to rake from the dying embers flashes of the stinging fires of hate, it were worse than time wasted. It was no fight of men with men. That is but brutality. It was the eternal war of right with wrong, which is divine and wreathes an eternal crown of glory round the brow of the conqueror. Our foes were not worth beating if the purpose were simply to beat them. But it was the chastisement of love that overthrew, not them, but the false gods they worshiped, the false principles they obeyed, and that gave to them and secured to us a union for the first time founded on universal freedom and equality. And so it is that as sometimes a brave man perils and loses his life that he may save that of a little child or even of a foe, so our heroes died that all their countrymen, North and South, might live the only life worth living, — the life of free men. It would be easy to say that the late war demonstrated that we are a nation of soldiers as well as of citizens, and to paint the laurels which, in case of another, we could win again on sea and land. But I prefer to say that the result is a united country, a solid South, such as it soon will be, only because at last and forever solidly identified with the education, the business growth, the glowing enterprise of the North, — its common people taught in common schools, its vast fields open to the stimulating immigration of the globe, its great rivers turning the wheels of peaceful and prosperous industries, — a united country that counts as nothing its ability to fight the world, but as everything its ability to lead the world in the arts of peace, secure in the consciousness rather than in the exhibition of power, and cemented not by blood but by ideas.

This is our triumph, — not that we overthrew a brave though ignorant, provincial, misguided foe, stunted by the barbarism of slavery, but that we have forever established in fact the principle that all men are born free and equal; have destroyed the doctrine of caste; have proved the stability and permanence of a government of the people; have consolidated our heterogeneous population and made them all of one birth and kin, so that the names of our fallen dead no longer, like those on the Lexington column, are all patronymics of pure New England stock, but, as you may now read them on the later shafts throughout the commonwealth, represent every nationality, each blending in the one common destiny of the American republic. We have confirmed the policy of honesty in financial administration, of keeping good the nation's promise, and of giving its people an honest dollar. We have struck the shackles from the feet of the slave and from the soul of his master. We have let loose the energies, the mighty energies of a free people, which are turning this great domain into a hive of industry and prosperity, girting it with bands of iron rails, and disemboweling its mines of gold and silver and more precious ores. Best of all, we have emancipated the prodigal States themselves from the swineherd's thraldom, and put rings on their hands and shoes on their feet, allowing them to justly share but never more to domineer. It was General Greene, of our neighbor Rhode Island, who a hundred years ago led South Carolina to victory in the War for Independence. It was General Lincoln, of our own Massachusetts, who received the sword of Cornwallis at Yorktown, in the same good cause. Since then, South Carolina and Virginia, false to that cause, have struck their flags to the men of Rhode Island and Massachusetts who held them to their better duty. They will not repeat that mistake. Within this month, at the centennial celebration at Cowpens, it was Colonel Higginson, a representative of the Massachusetts Executive, who spoke for New England on the same platform with General Hampton, whose slaves, less than twenty years ago, the colonel had armed against this their master, in the cause of their own liberty. And both struck the same high note of freedom, of progress, of the new era of a higher destiny. In October next, the soldiers of the North will again encamp at Yorktown. But it will be to celebrate, not the slaughters of the Peninsula campaign, but the hundredth anniversary of the achievement of American Independence. On that day, the President of the Union and the representatives of every State in it will look back over the century and pay tribute to its sacrifices and its triumphs. But with faces on which no shadow will fall, they will turn anon and look forward for centuries to come upon the more glorious fraternal progress of the future. It has been said that it would be better to blot out this day and with it every recollection of the past it commemorates. I believe it is better to keep the day and to forget nothing of the past, if so on both sides we make the past a lesson for the future, and out of its very nettle of horror and danger pluck the flower of safety. The mere man you fought is naught, and it is indeed better to forgive and forget him. But the victory you won over him was the victory of principle, and is eternal. Proud may you be indeed to keep it known that you share and transmit its glory; that, having as soldiers saved the republic, as citizens you perpetuate it; that you recall a youth not lost but made immortal. Proud, too, the Commonwealth of such sons; secure in their hands alike in peace or war; her motto still, THE QUIETUDE OF PEACE WITH LIBERTY BUT ELSE THE SWORD.

In that Commonwealth, her very soil rich with ashes of heroes and giants, fitting it is that you should not limit the honors you bestow this day to the graves only of the recent dead, but should extend them to the dead who for two hundred and fifty years have been, by force of their indelible impress, the real life, transcending ours, of Massachusetts. And fitting it is that I, echoing their sentiment and yours, the sentiment that never was ungenerous or narrow, should speak no word that is not liberal, no thought that is not national, no hope of future good that is not as broad as our common country, or that does not embrace the happiness of every citizen, whatever his color or birth, whatever his faith or toil, whatever his section or estate. For we commemorate to-day not more the heroism of the past than the common weal of the present, — the equality of citizenship, in honor commanding respect, in duty commanding service.

As I look, veterans, upon your faces, your thinner ranks, your brows on which time is writing in plainer lines its autograph, true, indeed, I know it is that the number of the survivors is fast diminishing, and that with the close of the century few will remain. But they will all still live in the works that do follow them, — in a civilization better because purified by the searching fire of war from the dross of human slavery and political inequality, and in a country lifted up to a higher plane of justice, mercy, and righteousness. They will live, too, in history, — in the history of a patriotic people, pictured in pages more graphic than those of Plutarch or Macaulay, in the songs of poets who shall sing a nobler than Virgil's man, and an epic loftier than the Iliad. They will live, too, in these monuments of stone and bronze which we erect not more to their memory than to the incitement and education of coming generations. It might be said that we are now in our monumental age. The towering obelisk at Bunker Hill, the homely pillar on Lexington Green, are no longer the only columns that write in granite the record of our glory. At Plymouth, the colossal figure of Faith, looking out over the sea, catching from its horizon the first tints of the morning, and guarding the graves of the Pilgrims, proclaims to the world the story of the Mayflower and its precious freight of civil and religious liberty. Across the bay rises almost to completion the plain but solid shaft that marks the home of Miles Standish, that sturdy type of courage and independence in life and faith which has been multiplied in New England in every phase of its thought and culture. In Boston, before the State House, Webster, defender of the Constitution, and Mann, the promoter of public education. Before its City Hall, Franklin, the most prolific and comprehensive brain in American history, and Quincy, a noble name in Massachusetts for generation after generation. In its public squares, Winthrop, the Puritan founder, Sam Adams, true leader of the people, and Abraham Lincoln, emancipator of the grateful race that kneels enfranchised at his feet. In its Public Garden, the equestrian statue of Father Washington, the figure of Charles Sumner, and the uplifted arm of Everett. And in its avenues, Hamilton, the youthful founder of our national finance, and John Glover, colonel of the Marblehead regiment, whose lusty arms and oars rescued Washington from Long Island. At Mount Auburn, James Otis, that flame of fire. At Lexington, Hancock and Adams. At Concord, the embattled farmer. In Hingham, in marble pure as his own heroic instincts, that war governor, who in the heart of the Massachusetts soldier can never be disassociated from the sympathies and martyrdom of the service which he shared with you even to his life. And now, in Chelsea, the national flag, floating out its bright and rippling cheer from the year's beginning to its end, waves over the Soldiers' Home, which has been secured by your contributions, so that if haply there be one needy veteran whom the magnificent and unparalleled provision of Massachusetts fails, as all general laws must, in some rare cases, fail to reach, there he may find a shelter that shall not dishonor him. Time and your patience would fail an enumeration of the monuments which, within a few years, have dotted the State, and in whose massive handwriting the century is recording for centuries hence its story of heroism, so plain, so legible, that though a new Babel should arise, and the English tongue be lost, the human heart and eye will still read it at a glance. Scarce a town is there — from Boston, with its magnificent column crowned with the statue of America, at the dedication of which even the conquered Southron came to pay honor, to the humblest stone in rural villages — in which these monuments do not rise summer and winter, in snow and sun, day and night, to tell how universal was the response of Massachusetts to the call of the patriots' duty, whether it rang above the city's din or broke the quiet of the farm. On city square and village green stand the graceful figures of student, clerk, mechanic, farmer, in that endeared and never-to-be-forgotten war uniform of the soldier or the sailor, their stern young faces to the front, still on guard, watching the work they wrought in the flesh, and teaching, in eloquent silence, the lesson of the citizen's duty to the state. How our children will study these! How they will search and read their names! How quaint and antique to them will seem their arms and costume! How they will gather and store up in their minds the fine, insensibly filtering percolation of the sentiment of valor, of loyalty, of fight for right, of resistance against wrong, just as we inherited all this from the Revolutionary era, so that, when some crisis shall in the future come to them, as it came to us, they will spring to the rescue, as sprang our youth in the beauty and chivalry of the consciousness of a noble descent.

During the late Turco-Russian war, I passed an evening in a modest home in a quiet country town. It was a wild night. The family circle sat by the open fire of a New England sitting-room. They told me of a son of that house, a young man already known in literature and art, who, full of the spirit of adventure, was at that moment, as war correspondent of a great London daily, with the head of the Russian army in Bulgaria. They read me his letters, in which he interwove affectionate inquiries and memories of home with vivid descriptions of battles, of wounds, of Turkish barbarities, of desolated villages, of murdered and mutilated peasants, of long marches through worse than Virginian mud, of wild bivouac in rain and tempest, of stirring incidents of the Russian camp, of the thousand shifting scenes of the theatre of a campaign, till suddenly that quiet room in which we sat was transfigured, and we, snug-sheltered from the storm, were apace translated over the sea into the very stir and toss of the war, our sympathies, our hopes, our interests, our very selves all there.

And so it is with us always. Shut up within ourselves, our minds intent on nothing but the narrow limits of immediate place and time, our hearts and fists closing tighter on our little own, we shrivel like dry leaves. But let the thrill of that common humanity electrify us which links together all men, all time past, present, and to come, and we spring into the upper air. When we do these honors to the deserving dead, when we revive not alone the fact but the ideal of their service, we strike a chord that forever binds us and the world around us with all great heroisms, with all great causes and sacrifices, with the throb of that loftier moral atmosphere which is lost only in the unison of man's immortal soul with the soul of God the Father.

ADDRESS

We have met in Faneuil Hall to consider, and, I trust, to act upon, the most appalling sudden disaster that has befallen any portion of the people of the United States. Ten thousand men, women, little children, — our country-men, our fellow human beings, akin to you and me by the passionate ties of human suffering and human sym-pathy, only yesterday busy and thrifty dwellers in a happy valley in the mountains of Pennsylvania, have been liter-ally swallowed up by the deluge, burned by the relentless flame, their homes actually blotted from the face of the earth, their families scattered, never to reunite, their charred bodies tossed broadcast or in heaps, while the survivors are left with broken hearts, sobbing through their tears, in the agonizing search to find the dead body of father, or mother, or child, or little babe. Where but a day ago there was plenty, where there was comfortable shelter, where there was every provision, where honest labor was earning a generous return, to-day gaunt famine stalks, children are crying for food and seeking shelter from the cold and the rain; and this paradise of labor has no vestige left except its own ruins and its ghastly population of corpses. Why, the heart gasps in speech-less horror at such a scene as this, which breaks upon the even tenor of our general national felicity. No words can describe it, and well it is they cannot, for the question now is, not what shall we say, but what shall we do.

As I came in it struck me that there are two great overwhelming feelings that come over one at such a time as this. One is the thought of the utter insignificance of this human body, this man, this pigmy creature that struts and frets for his hour, and yet at one convulsion of the dead clod on which he walks, and which he spurns under his foot, at one freak of those mighty natural forces which play with him and then in an unguarded moment tear him, at one breath of Almighty God, is tossed like a leaf and flung like an atom in a dust heap. But the next thought and the greater thought, thanks to the same Almighty power, is the significance and the value and the worth of the human soul. The floods and deluge may break their bonds and carry ruin in their track; yet though they devastate the valley and the hillside and remove mountains, if they do but so much as touch one of God's little ones; if but a sparrow of a babe do fall under their ruin; if, as in a case like this, there is a holocaust of men and women like ourselves and like those whom we hold dear, then there speeds a thrill that is finer than any electric force which nature supplies. It is the thrill of the human heart. A chord, that reaches through angels' hearts to the heart of God himself, is touched. Then any cry of human suffering, be it ever so faint, is heard above the roar of the mighty waters, and above the fury of the hissing flames; and then, too, the glad answer of relief is also heard echoing back in helpful response. Then it is that man becomes mightier than nature, because man is master of matter; and we are taught, as perhaps nothing but such an awful calamity as this could teach us, we are taught our common humanity, — shall I not say we are taught our common divinity, of course our common citizenship and brotherhood, and our common obligations to those who now are not so much our countrymen as they are our brothers, our sisters, in suffering.

It is in that spirit that this meeting is called. It is in that spirit that you all have responded to-day. It is in that spirit that the men and women of good, old, generous Boston, heart of Massachusetts, her merchants, her working men and women, those who have much and those who have little, have come together to unite to carry succor and sympathy and help to these sufferers at Johnstown, — food for the hungry, clothing for the naked, shelter for the homeless, and a balm for the wounds of those on whom the most awful calamity of the century has just fallen.

RESPONSE

IF any one will tell me the difference between Universalism and Unitarianism, I shall be able, as I am not now, to see why I may not claim a seat at your denominational banquet as a matter of right ·and of membership in your faith, if not in your club. Your firm name is a little broader and more comprehensive, — comprehensive enough, Dr. Miner will allow, to include even a poor, despised Republican. You have monopolized the most generous word in the English language. But when it comes to the essentials, — to the fatherhood of God and the brotherhood of man, — to the doctrine of the ultimate holiness and happiness of all God's children, — to the faith that there is a better life for us all, not only worth having, but to be had here and hereafter, if striven for, — in all these things we stand on a common platform. And, between you and me, the whole intelligent world is coming to stand there, too, without much other distinction of sect than so far as relates to the fashion of the mould, the extent of the ritual, the mere form of expression. The recent conference of churches at Hartford is a recognition of two things: first, that the old-time doctrinal differences are pretty well obliterated, preserved only in the lingual ruts of words which keep half alive the husk of a term long after its meaning has evaporated; and, second, that the Christian church has now enough to do in maintaining against the world those fundamentals of Christianity on which all sects agree, without wasting its energies in the wrangles of its own subdivisions.

I am told to-day that it is just a hundred years since, in 1785, the first convention of Universalist ministers and parishes was held, thus constituting the germ of your present general convention. During that time what growth have you not had; what missionary work have you not done ; where have you not carried the banner of your liberal faith; in what corner of the country have you not dropped the seed of your church, your colleges, your academies, your literature, — multiplying a hundred fold their influence not only within but outside of your strict denominational lines? With what philanthropy and reform have you not been associated? In view of these things, there are certainly two reasons why we of the laity should be glad to sit at your festival. In the first place, it gives us an opportunity to pay the respect we so cordially feel to the body of the clergy who, no longer relying on the artificial stagings of the ministerial office, or of an establishment, stand for the truths of Christian faith and Christian morals, and are still the unfailing fountain of good influences and good teaching. There are black sheep in every flock, even among the laity, but when I think of the great body of the ministry of all sects, of their devotion to the work of making the world better, of their stimulus to a higher and diviner life, of their toil and sacrifice, of the usually small return to them of the good things of this world, and of their faithful service these many years, I am happy to add my small voice in appreciation of their beneficence. For I find them identified with the cause of education in its broadest sense, cherishing the schools, promoting temperance, searching out the unfortunate and poor, dispensing charity, the almoners of sympathy, and, after all, still as of yore, one of the strong reliances of our New England system.

In the second place, this festival occasion, bringing together the clergy and the laity, suggests what is, indeed, the main thing, — the fact that our interest is a common one. You of the clergy are not of one jurisdiction, and we of the laity of another. We are all of the same fold, only with convenient subdivisions of labor. These days, like all days in the history of mankind heretofore and forevermore, are crucial and decisive days. The problem of life is never solved, and yet the method of its solution is as plain as daylight. And that method is progress, progress, progress, — progress in physical and material circumstance, in intellectual enlargement and force, in moral sentiment, in æsthetic refinement, in personal character. To all these our religious faith and culture are the in-and-through running thread that makes their fibre. The school, the church, the press, — in short, every institution of modern progress is an agency in their development. But close at their heels sweeps the threatening tide of demoralization and rot and sin and shame and vice and misery, and the issue is always the same, whether the Red Sea shall swallow all up, or the Promised Land be reached. It is a conflict that at once stirs to the most heroic endeavor, and at the same time promises the reward of the truest and noblest victory. And it is because this occasion and this outlet of your denominational zeal command clergy and laity to one common duty in this respect, that it is fitting we should thus gather together in consecration anew to the keeping of the faith and the fighting of the good fight.

Personally, I am happy to be here. I recall my acquaintance during my public and private life with so many of your representative men and women. I recall the June Commencement days and the spreading tent at Tufts Hill, where Capen teaches, and where I still seem to hear the sonorous voice and see the front lock fluttered by the breeze on the forehead of Israel Washburn. I recall the ministrations in the town of my own residence of Brother Livermore, and the inspiration now and then of the eloquence, or better than eloquence, the wisdom, of his wife, that evangel of good teaching, Mary Livermore. I recall the hard blows, some of which I have had to take, but with many of which I cordially sympathize, of that fearless champion whom I always name with respect, Dr. Miner. I recall from out of my earliest recollection the voice of Streeter, and, in later youth, the declamation of Chapin. And especially do I look back to the sunrise of my own life, and the religious instruction of my childhood, — the little Maine village nestling in the hills; the only meeting-house in it a Universalist house of worship; the constant if not brilliant elder who eked out the shadow, or rather the shadow of a shadow, of a salary, by keeping the winter school and grubbing the small parochial acre; the unpainted pews; the open windows (for in my memory it was unending summer time) through which my eyes went always wandering; the drowsy hum outside of insect life, more slumberous even than the preacher's voice; the still dreamier haze of an atmosphere of eternal sunshine veiling the sky and tempering the lights and shadows on the hills and fields; the hard-working farmers who, in clean Sunday cotton, sat in their shirt sleeves, closing their eyes, not in irreverence, but in a sacred rest that I am sure was entirely acceptable to the

Good Father; and all the rural and now so tender memories of that day. Ah, my friends, when so much of the
poetry of life is in its memories, in the associations of
childhood, in the search for the red strawberry and the
yellow buttercup, is it not something that we of New
England, we of country birth, we of these kindly liberal
faiths, can recall our Scripture, our Sunday-school lessons,
our Bible verses, our sacred songs, our Sabbath hymns,
and the whole aroma of our early religious lore from the
resources of a faith that is inspired by the sunshine of
God's universal love, by the hope and not the terror of
his judgment, by the ultimate holiness and not the ultimate degradation, the redemption, not the casting out, the
unity, not the separation here or hereafter, of all his
children, — weak in their shortcomings, but immortal in
their aspirations.

ADDRESS

To the Colored Veterans in the Hingham Cemetery,
August 2, 1887.

I wish I had the power to utter the inexpressible emotions I feel in the presence of these representatives of a race which was the cause of the war, yet not by any means the least potent and patriotic influence in bringing it to a successful close. It is a scene which touches the heart, and revives sacred memories. We can feel, but we cannot utter them. Mine is a lighter duty, the duty in behalf of the town of Hingham, where Governor Andrew made his summer home, to welcome you to this spot in which he lies buried. You have come with tender and loving regard to decorate his grave. The skies yesterday shone upon you in the gladness of your reunion. They are not false to-day; they only mingle their tears with yours over this sacred soil.

If he could rise from it, if he were here,— if, indeed, he be not here, — think for a moment on what his eyes would rest. Surely he would behold more, infinitely more than even his fervid and hopeful enthusiasm — that enthusiasm which inspired the Commonwealth, inspired the country, and inspired you — ever pictured or dared to forecast. For he would behold these representatives of the millions of a race who were in bondage only a generation ago, but among whom to-day, thanks to him, thanks to men like him, thanks to yourselves, no fetter clanks through the length and breadth of the land. He would behold them, not merely redeemed from bondage, but citizens, like himself, of our great republic, endowed by constitutional amendment with full right of suffrage, holding state and national office, members of Congress, graduates of our schools and universities, leaders of public opinion, ranking in the professions, gaining in the accumulation of wealth in the very States where, twenty-five years ago, they were under the yoke, and thus destined to become a conservative force in the future of our national life.

Best of all is this, that they have arrived in this short time to such measure that the only word which seems unfitting at this time is the word which in any way refers to them as a separate or distinctive people, or as anything else than American citizens.

The great heart that has crumbled into ashes here would never have been satisfied with any narrower designation than that. Ah! my friends, how that heart beat for you! Its consecration to you illuminated his face, it made his tongue ring like a bugle, it made his pen fire, and his will iron. Never, indeed, will you forget John Albion Andrew. You were his friends, and he laid down his life for you. He did his work, he kept the faith, he fought the fight, he finished the course. If I might intrude any word on you, it would be, that your flowers, however fragrant, your songs, however sweet, are not the best tribute of this hour; your tears, however quick, nor your eloquence, however fervid. But you owe him this, — to go on in that same faith and fight and course in which he led and in which you have followed, relying no longer on exterior help, relying upon your own souls, the value of each of which he recognized and the whole war was fought for, — to go on fulfilling the faith, the fight, the course of the true man, the free citizen, the self-poised, self-reliant, self-respecting, self-ennobling son of God, mastering your opportunities, enlarging your education, and still marching on, even as the soul of John Brown goes marching on.

RESPONSE

I TAKE it, Mr. President, that the true end of a good State is to so help its people and its institutions as quickest to enable them to take care of themselves. This result has certainly been achieved in respect to Harvard, which now not only stands alone, but has achieved its best work in its present condition of entire independence. In kindly pursuance of an ancient courtesy, the governor of the Commonwealth is indeed called up at your annual board to respond in her behalf. But I know that the time has come when it is only to do these three things: first, still in pursuance of the ancient custom, to exhibit to you the subdued glitter of his staff and the red coats of the Lancers; second, to bring you her congratulations, her expression of confidence in your present work, and her thanks for your great contributions to education and patriotism ; and, third, to join with you in extending a welcome to the guests who come from foreign lands or from sister States, and, let me add, at this time, — may such another occasion not soon occur,— to join in your regret at the separation from Harvard of that beloved pastor, who has reflected not more credit upon the college than upon the Commonwealth. If it happens, as it does to-day, that her representative is also one of your own graduates, not only does he do this duty with a warm personal interest, but the comparison which his own memory

enables him to make between the spirit and the work of
this university, as it was and as it is, is itself an enthusiastic tribute to its recent progress and increased beneficence.
Time was, as perhaps it always must be, when almost the
only inspiration was in the student's heart. Whatever
came to him came, as perhaps must always be the case,
more as an incident than as a result. But now, surely,
the people of the Commonwealth have a satisfaction, never
greater than to-day, in the bearing and fruit of Harvard,
because, under its present administration, it is lifted out
of those ruts which are never a thing of the past, but
which grow every year like the wrinkles on the horn of
an ox; and because it is under a leader who has made the
college felt in every fibre of the life of the state, and who
from the outer world, which constantly owes something to
his voice and suggestion, draws also back still more to
freshen and fit the youth of Harvard for the world's work.
The whole cause of education is strengthened. The whole
domain of youth is enlarged. The scholar is indeed made
a power. President Eliot in thus recognizing the broader
needs and the best elements of that body of the people,
which is Massachusetts, pays them, if an unconscious, yet
a just, tribute. And they in turn pay him the tribute of
their appreciation. If he were in the political arena, I
am quite sure he would afford that combination, referred
to by the young orator of the morning, whose theme was
the eighth President of the United States, — the combination of intellectual strength and skill in affairs.

For the Commonwealth no response is needed, certainly
not in this presence of her sons, who are themselves her
best response. The pessimists, who always go mad with
the summer heats or possibly now at the approach of the
comet, who always find so much to criticise in the spots

on the sun that they make the sun itself a failure, and who draw all their saws and instances from that metropolis from which you, sir, are glad to escape now and then to the purer air of Massachusetts, would find their occupation gone, were they to take up their abode in her borders. Corruption may stalk, but not in her legislative halls. Money may buy offices, but has not yet bought hers; indeed the income of her officials is less than that of the average college professor. The price of her judiciary is at least above rubies, as well it may be, for that is the price of wisdom. Her civil service, Mr. Curtis, is not the worst on the face of the globe. Life, liberty, and the pursuit of happiness are ensured. Property is secure. Order prevails. Industry thrives. Charity abounds. Her prisons are asylums. Evidences of soul can be found, without the aid of the microscope, in her corporations. Her lawyers earn a modest fee. Her physicians meet in happy conclave and celebrate a century of respectable and kindly blundering. At all her centennials, — and they are becoming painfully frequent, — whether of town, or school, or society, or of whatever department of her life, no praises are quite loud enough to sing the excellence of her progress, till, going the rounds, perfection is found to be the condition of every institution except the unhappy one of politics, which is made a scapegoat for all the rest. And yet our politics are so far harmless. In her lexicon there is no such word as boss. Her people have no "leader." They have their way and get what they want in the choice of their candidates far more than in that of their sermons, or, as the statistics begin to show, of their marriages. But the price of all this is vigilance. There is danger — danger from greed, danger from intolerance and narrowness above and ignorance below, danger from lack of that generous culture which lifts a man to the exercise of the best things in himself and to the appreciation of the best things in his fellow men. And to meet this danger the Commonwealth still looks to the training, the influence, the inspiration of her institutions of education; and to none more than to Harvard, which still is, as from the beginning it has been, at the head.

OPENING ADDRESS

At the Fair of the Society for the Prevention of Cruelty to Children, Horticultural Hall, Boston, December 8, 1880.

This fair is now open and will be held in aid of the Society for the Prevention of Cruelty to Children. As we·think of the faces of the little ones, at the sight of whom the heart of the Master melted so tenderly ; as we think of the little heads that under our own lamplight bow at nightfall in prayer, of the little hands that nestle in ours, of the eyes that laugh in happiness or droop when sickness comes; as we think at once of the dependence and priceless worth and sacredness of the soul of a little child, it seems incredible that there should be need of such a society, or that there should be such a thing as cruelty to children. And yet the record of Mr. Fay's work will show you instance after instance of neglect and outrage, of wrong to the soul and to the body, of exposure and blows and mutilation, of starvation and brutality, and also of the moral degradation that comes from the forcing of children into every species of imposture, deceit, and crime. It is not poverty that is at fault. Poverty is as tender and loving and devoted to its young as is wealth, and deserves credit far more, because it is tenderness, love, and devotion at far greater cost and sacrifice. It is the fault of crime and avarice, of fiendishness, and, more than all else, of the terrible and blunting savageness of strong drink and intoxication. The society to which I have re-

ferred, made up as it is of the union of two former societies, organized under the laws of the Commonwealth,
directed by some of your wisest and most philanthropic
citizens, and with an agent of great experience, humanity,
and skill, is endeavoring to search out the victims of such
wrong, to bring light to the desolate hearts of children
dependent and neglected, to relieve their immediate distress by improving their surroundings, or by helping to
transfer them to better ones, and especially to aid in
directing them into channels of education, honest labor,
and honest growth. It is a society that has no funds. It
depends entirely on the donations of the private citizen.
So far these have not failed, but the field is so broad, the
appeal is so touching, that this fair is held and the warm
heart of Massachusetts is besought to give yet more gen-
erously, so that a greater bounty may be bestowed and a
greater good done. Whatever the cause that is at your
hearts, — if it be education, here you may begin at its foundation; if it be the crusade against intemperance, here
you may rescue its victims from the earliest blight; if it
be the suppression of crime, here you may not only save
those who are exposed to its infliction, but snatch from
the path of temptation those who would otherwise grow
up to be its perpetrators. It appeals to the conscience
and prudence of men who feel the need of keeping the
social fabric wholesome and safe; — to the hearts of women, whom may Heaven bless for this and for many another charity, and to whom the most plaintive appeal on
earth is a child's cry of pain or a child's outstretched and
pleading hands, — and to the very happiness of those
favored children who, of all the blessings that fortune
showers upon them, cannot too soon learn that there is
none so sweet as the power to help others. There is no

literature, there are no songs so tender and touching as those which tell of the sympathies, the sorrows, the outreach of childhood. There will be no question of the fitness of your giving in this cause. Your gift, however light, will come back to you unconsciously, day after day, in the story of the rescue of some castaway group of little breaking hearts, in the face of some child brightened you know not how, in the manly life of some boy moving on in the honor and success of a true citizen, who but for the impulse of the charity to which this society and this fair are trying to give practical direction, might have been the criminal or the pauper, undermining or burdening society and the state. It may be yours to say some day with the poet, —

> " And thanks untraced to lips unknown
> Shall greet me like the odors blown
> From unseen meadows newly mown,
> Or lilies floating in some pond,
> Wood-fringed, the wayside gaze beyond ;
> The traveller owns the grateful sense
> Of sweetness near, he knows not whence,
> And pausing takes with forehead bare
> The benediction of the air."

And perhaps on your ears may sometime fall the blessed words : " Inasmuch as ye have done it unto one of the least of these, ye have done it unto me."

GENERAL GRANT.

AT THE MIDDLESEX CLUB DINNER, HOTEL BRUNSWICK,
OCTOBER 18, 1880.

I DEEM it my good fortune that it is permitted me in behalf of the Commonwealth of Massachusetts to bring, in few but sincere words, the hearty, cordial, unstinted greeting of all her people, whatever their color, whatever their birth, whatever their politics, rich or poor, — we have no high or low, — to that distinguished citizen who, however many other titles he may have earned or may hereafter earn in his varying and distinguished service of his country, will never be known by any title more enduring or more endearing than by that of General Grant. The people of Massachusetts honor him because he was a loyal soldier in war and because he is a loyal citizen in peace. I believe that there is no heart within our borders that has not beat quicker for his coming. There is no roof here, entering which he shall not find hanging on its walls, familiar as the face of Washington, the picture of the hero of Vicksburg, of Chattanooga, of Appomattox. If to-morrow or next day he shall fare through our rich autumnal scenery, his eye will fall upon many a modest headstone that marks the last resting-place of some one of those soldiers who loved him and followed him. If he tarry for never so short a time in any of our villages, the old veterans of the war will cluster around him to catch another grasp of the hand, another glimpse of the face of the man under whom they were willing to march to glory, and to follow on that line if it took all summer.

Above all partisanship, Massachusetts greets him here, because he was the general who never whined or flinched; because as President his veto saved the country from financial chaos; because as an American citizen, after receiving the most flattering attention at home and abroad, he has preserved his simplicity of character and only broadened into a nobler statesmanship and a wider faith in republican institutions; and perhaps most of all, because as a simple citizen, wise, disinterested, and patriotic in his recent utterances during the present year, he has shown, as an observer of the institutions of his country, a magnanimity which was large enough to take in not a part but the whole of it.

I should not do justice to the Commonwealth, also, if I did not greet him as the representative of the great West, which has been so largely peopled from the loins of Massachusetts and attuned by its spirit. If to-morrow he shall lay his ear above the graves of Bradford and Brewster and Winslow and Carver, and of that other doughty little captain, Miles Standish, he will distinguish, amid the music of the ocean which resounds at his feet, the strains of the finer music of those departed souls. It will breathe to him that love of liberty, that independence of individuality, that equality of all God's children, that eternal sense of right which, planted two hundred and fifty years ago on the icy and barren edge of Plymouth Rock, are to-day the most magnificent harvests of the West, richer than its grain and its gold, mightier even than its men of battle. I say that it will breathe that strain in his ear. As I remember his life and services, as I have read and as I have heard his words, I am sure that that strain has already been breathed to him. I deem it fortunate to-day that he, his family, and his friends come among us in the glorious season of the turning year. Our rivers and hillsides never more brilliant, our clear autumnal lights never more mellow, give him welcome. They give him welcome because he recalls that group of statesmen — some of them now glittering among the stars this October night — who stood for the salvation of our country in its great hour of peril; because he recalls to us Lincoln, who leaned on him; because he recalls Andrew, who looked not in vain to him to strike a blow; and because in so many loyal hearts and patriotic memories he stands as the representative of that loyalty which is more vital and more sacred even than loyalty to the flag, — loyalty to free government of the people, and to human rights. I am sure General Grant will take as the best word I can say that Massachusetts, in whatever other respects it honors him, honors him most in so far as he has fought for and stood for, and will continue to give the great weight of his influence to those ideals to the memory of which she rears these statues of Winthrop and Adams and Webster and Andrew, to the defense of which she sent Whitney and Shaw and Ladd and Lowell to die in the streets of Baltimore or on the battlefield, and for the maintenance of which she will hold all public men till she shall cease to be the Commonwealth of the Pilgrim and the Puritan.

GENERAL SHERMAN.

I THANK you, Mr. President, and through you the Merchants' Association of Boston, not only for this kindly
greeting, but also for the opportunity to pay my personal
respects to General Sherman, and to convey to him from
the whole Commonwealth a " Merry Christmas " and a
" Happy New Year." Yes, Mr. President, many and
many a happy new year of a long and useful life ! I had
hoped to do him what I might modestly call the greatest
honor of his life by receiving him under the gilded dome,
by introducing him to our military and civil officials, to my
staff, also gilded, and particularly to our honorable councilors, one of whom, I believe, has the still greater honor of
being a member of the Merchants' Association ; by reading
to him a portion of my forthcoming inaugural address ; by
pointing his reverential gaze to the sacred codfish, and,
certainly, by touching his heart and dimming his eyes, as
I know they would have been dimmed, at the sight in
Doric Hall of our regimental flags, some of which have
often bent to salute him in the field, and beneath which
so many of the soldiers of Massachusetts, with never-
failing confidence in their commander, have followed him
into the fire of battle, and have tramped with him from
Atlanta to the sea. And if he had stayed to listen I am
not sure that he would not have heard, faint from their
folds at first, but soon loud and stirring upon his ear, a

familiar strain as ten thousand loyal voices came back to his memory, singing the resounding chorus of "Marching through Georgia."

While I regret that he has been obliged to decline me this, yet I very much rejoice that it is because the extension of other courtesies to him by our citizens has preoccupied his time, so that he needs no added assurance of how welcome he is everywhere among our people, and how universal and sincere is their appreciation of his great services. The people of Massachusetts, general, are a patriotic people. Love of country is in the very fibre of their hearts. They breathe it in the air ; they are taught it in every verse they sing, in every public word they hear, and in every line they read. They honor the flag in defense of which their best blood has run, and they are loyal to the republic which their best brains and conscience helped to found, to better, and to perpetuate. But their love of country is large enough and generous enough to embrace it all. They value the triumph of the national arm, in wielding which you had so large a share, mainly in proportion as it has opened a greater opportunity for the common progress of the whole country. And therefore they especially honor a man who to brilliant service in the field, — to a conqueror's march through an enemy's country as famous now, both in itself and in its commander's story of its progress, as that of Xenophon, — and to a final victory second only to that of Richmond, could also add the magnanimity of generous terms to a surrendering foe, and who, from that day to this, has known nothing narrower than a reunited country. In behalf, therefore, of the Commonwealth, I extend most cordial greeting to General Sherman.

Nor, certainly, can I do that, especially in the presence

of the merchants of Boston, without calling to mind another of the same name and of the same blood, who, in civil life, has distinguished himself equally with our honored guest in his military career. Massachusetts knows no better financial philosophy than an honest dollar, the best money for all alike, and the exact payment of every public obligation. And, grateful to the Secretary of the Treasury for his splendid administration of this branch of the government upon these simple principles, she only hopes that his successor will be as good a man as John Sherman himself.

If Massachusetts were to give you a toast, therefore, I am sure she would give you The Two Shermans, — William and John. With their kinsman, Roger, they form a constellation in the public service of their country. Indeed we may regard them as our Castor and Pollux, — one the tamer of that fiery steed, the greenback, and the other a boxer, whose gauntlet was an army corps of freemen fighting for the integrity of the whole country, for the emancipation of the slave, and for the emancipation, also, even of their foes from the barbarism and palsy of ownership in man.

GENERAL LOGAN.

In behalf of the Commonwealth from which I come, I am glad to join in this tribute to the brave and loyal soul, without fear and without reproach, the soldier's idol and friend, the founder of Memorial Day, — General Logan. We pay our tribute, not to his memory, but to him. It is the poverty of our language, if not of our thoughts, that when men die we speak of them as gone, and inscribe our honors to their memories rather than to their immortal lives.

General Logan was rarely in New England. Only a small fraction of our people ever saw him. But for that very reason he is scarcely more gone from them now than he was during his earthly walk. Then, as now, he was, and now, as then, he is to them a life ; a positive force added to the world's dynamic energies ; an impulse of patriotism ; a factor in the national vitality ; a suggestion of personal courage, of loyal service, of public and private integrity ; a type of characteristic American citizenship. He has fixed himself upon their vision like a star.

The scenes of the war exhibit no more vivid picture than that which one of his eulogists in the House of Representatives gave of him at Atlanta on the 22d of July, 1864, when McPherson was slain, the Army of Tennessee was falling back, and Logan, its new commander, mounted on his black war-horse, his hair floating back, his eyes ablaze, his voice ringing like a bugle, came, like Sheridan at Winchester, flashing down the line which, rallying at his lead, returned to the attack, and drove the foe from the field. Nor was there ever a nobler magnanimity than his toward Thomas.

For these reasons a peculiarly warm and effusive regard always springs toward him from the hearts of the people. To them he was the black eagle of victory. If they or their press ever criticised him, they never doubted him. If, in the fiery contentions of our politics, they charged him with the faults which are the common lot of all, they never questioned the strong, heroic qualities he shared, not with all, nor even with the many, but with the few. He was not the greatest soldier of the war, yet he stands its most picturesque and striking volunteer, never failing in promptness or performance. He was not the first statesman of the republic, yet he was one of the moulding forces that shaped its political course. He was not the foremost of orators, yet he exerted an influence on public sentiment which the most eloquent orators might envy. It may be said of him, which cannot be said of others who have ranked higher, that he never fell below himself or the expectation which was had of him. His military career was far greater and more brilliant than his training or his opportunity would have suggested. There was no coming short of himself, no disappointment to the hope.

He again represents, as so many have represented, that splendid type of American improvement of American opportunities. His were frontier life, obstacles, struggle, courage, persistence, indefatigable industry, quenchless ambition, success, victory, and the desert of victory. In the generations to come the American boy's heart, as he learns his country's story, will burn with the picture of the martial figure and achievements of John A. Logan. The posterity of the emancipated slaves will remember his loyalty to their race, — fighting in war for their freedom, and in peace for their equal rights before the law. And the American fireside will long recall, as an inspiring stimulus to the purity and blessedness of home, the domestic bond that united him and Mary, his wife, hardly more together than it united them both in the respect of their countrymen and countrywomen.

It was his distinction that he emphasized the talents God gave him. The whole republic recognizes him as a conspicuous example; as one of its heroes, not of exaggeration, but of the great body of the people; not of romance, but of our realistic American life. As such the people loved him; as such we pay him here and now our tribute, grateful for his services in war and peace, his chivalrous courage, his pure, brave, patriotic life. Still with us are Sherman and Sheridan; over the river are Grant, Thomas, Hancock, Logan, and so many, many illustrious names of captains and privates. All these are now of one equal rank at last in God's grand army and loyal legion.

RESPONSE

AT THE BANQUET OF THE NATIONAL DRUGGISTS' ASSOCIATION AT
ODD FELLOWS HALL, BOSTON, AUGUST 25, 1887.

IT is very little I can say in response to your toast except to thank you for my seat at your generous board in this goodly company. If the variety from which I have supped is a sample of your wares, then I am sure your drugs are very delightful to take; and the price, a few words in the way of a speech, is much more reasonable than your general reputation would lead one to believe. I feel something of kinship with you, when I remember that the ordinary congressman's speech is one of the commonest drugs in the market. But none the less disinterestedly can I testify to the debt which the whole community owe you. Why, sir, more than half the literature and most of the pictorial charm in the daily papers — need I refer to their advertising columns? — are yours. Disinterested and spontaneous lovers of their fellow men pour their confessions into the public prints so that others may learn, as they have learned, that all the ills to which the human body is heir fly at your approach; that where one spear of hair once grew, there now grow two; that grim dyspepsia is only the dark portal which opens upon the luxurious vista of its cure; and that the kidneys are but a providential agency for tickling the palate with nectars such as were never dreamed of by the gods. You have added a new picturesqueness to nature with the blazonry which your Raphaels and Angelos — Mike Angelos — have daubed on every cliff and rural barn. My earliest instruction in art, when, a boy in Maine, I bought candy in a country store, was to gaze with large eyes upon the illustrated placard which, specked somewhat by the summer flies, but still gaudily picturing the wall, portrayed the glory and beneficence of Townsend's Sarsaparilla. It is said that Daniel Webster took his first lesson in statesmanship from studying the Constitution printed on a cheap pocket-handkerchief. We are like him in this respect, many of us having had our early reading lessons in deciphering the directions, in large type, on the label of Perry Davis' Pain Killer. What brings such sweet somnolence as a drug, — unless it be a sermon? Where else than at the druggists' do you find such a charming and efficient cure for all ills, — except in the solemn platform of a political party convention?

As a Massachusetts man I gladly join in welcoming to Boston you who have come from the cities of the whole country over. There is no extent to which the "Hub" will not go in yielding every courtesy to her sister cities. If she fail at all in that respect, attribute it to her modest reluctance to surpass them in their previous receptions of your association. You have given me rather an indefinite toast, "Our Representatives in Congress." As one of them I am of course your friend, and thank you for calling me so. Why, sir, what Congressman, looking at yet higher honors, would not be the friend of five hundred adults, voters, representing so many States of the Union, each one with a ballot in his hand, each having paid his poll-tax, although at the same time evading as much of the rest of his tax as he conveniently can? I speak not for myself, but rather for the whole general membership of that distinguished legislative body to which you have referred, when I say that, clumsy, uncertain, and slow as may be the steps of Congress, yet Congress does desire and try, as far as possible, to look after and attend to your business interests and the general interests of the country. I recall the frequent pathetic, if not poetic, picture of dignified and venerable gentlemen, whom in private life you could not touch with a ten-foot pole, if, peradventure, you should ever desire to touch them with a ten-foot pole, who yet, when once elected to service in Washington, become the most servile of errand boys, sweating through the departments to do chores for the people whom they represent and whose suffrages they are willing, not on their own account, but yielding to the demand of their "friends," to retain. You ask, why then does not Congress do something, why not pass this law or that? The answer is, because of the great conflict of interests among you and in the community at large. Congress is only the expression of public sentiment, — nothing more. If that public sentiment is divided, Congress is divided. When that sentiment unites to the extent of a majority sentiment, then Congress enacts its commands. You say you want a bankrupt law and can get none. It is because there is not a sufficient majority of people in favor of it to secure its passage. You have not had, since 1883, a revision of the tariff. It is because public sentiment has not been united enough in demanding it. In other words, it is you, and other associations like yours, who, not as individuals, but as the great business constituencies of the nation, are the real Congress of the United States. The responsibility is yours as well as ours. It is for you to mould the public sentiment and pay the bills ; for us to formulate it into law and draw the salary.

In all seriousness, gentlemen, I should not do myself or

this occasion justice if I did not speak my word of tribute to the beneficence and importance of your guild. You represent millions of accumulated and invested capital. You employ thousands and thousands of employees. You distribute uncounted wages, which is the material bread of life. You turn the wheels of manufactories, and spread the sails, and weight the iron steeds of commerce. Thus from your own arena you reach into swift and vital relations with every social, political, and industrial problem, and becoming more than members of your own department of activity, are efficient and responsible forces in the great onward civilization of the age. Nor do I forget that there is in you something of the Good Samaritan, who poured the oil and wine; and that your work goes to the assuaging of human suffering, the finding of new and more helpful agencies for securing health and repelling disease, and to the holding up of the hands of the physician and surgeon, whose ministry is akin to that of him who ministers to the sorrows and needs of the human soul. You have the sweetest of all rewards, the consciousness of helping humanity; of somehow, somewhere, making some one happier and better by bringing sleep to a tired eyelid, by bringing rest to an exhausted brain, by bringing quiet to a shattered and tingling nerve, by bringing relief to pain, cure to disease, health to infirmity, and by bringing also, let you and me frankly say, a modest profit in return to your pockets, and now and then a good dinner to a poor but respectable congressman.

WEBSTER CENTENNIAL

A HUNDRED years ago last January Daniel Webster
was born. Thirty years ago this month he died and was
buried on this farm. To-day we visit his grave, not
pouring upon it libations of wine and milk and blood, not
shedding over it the tears of recent grief, but paying it
the tribute of a reverent memory, the gratitude of a
nation's heart, and the justice due a mighty defender and
saviour of our country. My poor word of praise and criticism concerning him has been spoken, and I shall not
repeat it. Here he speaks for himself. On this sacred
soil, within sight of these elms, in the open air of this
October day, there comes a feeling that he is here, that
his great eyes greet us, and that his eloquent lips will
speak and silence ours. And here, indeed, he is. What
idle formality was it that took us to the dust he long ago
shook off, when here, in every whisper of the wind, in
every scarlet leaf, in these woods and fields and streams,
he, the genius of them all, still lives, as he still lives
in the constitution he expounded and moulded, in the
union he cemented and preserved, and in the impress he
stamped upon the political sentiment of the American
people.

This spot has been well chosen for the tribute of this
day. Here, with a sense of restfulness and sympathy,
came the great heart of Daniel Webster. Large as was
the honor he bestowed on Marshfield, he bestowed nothing

grander than he found. For here the lonely sea, which he loved, and in whose vastness and grandeur his own great soul felt a subtle kinship, communed with him, yet spoke no language he did not comprehend, and breathed no whisper he did not catch. Here with him the pilgrim sage sought the freedom of the new world for the exercise of his conscience. Here Winslow and Standish and Bradford and Brewster walked the forest aisles and discussed with him great themes of constitutional law, of chartered rights, of civil and religious liberty. Here, under his elm and from beneath his almost equally overhanging brim and brow, he saw the sails of the Mayflower far off, and in her cabin gravely drew the compact that embodied the germ of those basal ideas of union and liberty, one and inseparable, which were imprinted on his heart like a legend. Here in all the earth and air was the spirit of that pilgrim enterprise and purpose of which he never tired, to which he drew close, and from which he drank copious inspiration. Here, too, the very soil, responding to his sympathetic care and nurture, turned to verdure and beauty ; here he looked his oxen in the face ; and here the wide fields, barren and bleak, clothed themselves for him with the graceful shade of groves and were musical with the rustle of the waving grain. In the touching homely humanity which attaches to Webster in his relation to rural things, to the farm and to all the instincts of neighborly New England life, there is something that endears him to us, independent of his great eminence as a statesman and a lawyer. Whether he planted, or fished, or gunned, or waded streams, or cooled his shadowy brow under the trees, or drove over the country roads, or met his neighbors in the fields or by the fireside, it was still the same ; it was the sense of the proximity of a New England man, born in the humble farmhouse, true to the instincts of the fields, and loving the cattle and the hay, the furrow and the marsh.

And here the great orator, the great senator, the great lawyer, is still the Marshfield farmer and neighbor. He has to-day given us all a cordial welcome. He has fed us at his table. He has sat with us in his library and under his elm. He has shown us his crops and barns, his cattle and sheep. We grasp his hand and go back to our homes, and not till we have broken the charm of his personal courtesy are we fully conscious that we have been with him who pronounced the magnificent funeral oration of Adams and Jefferson, the discourses at Plymouth Rock and Bunker Hill, the Dartmouth College argument, and the overwhelming and resistless replies to Hayne and Calhoun. All honor to his memory ; all gratitude for his service ; all justice to his fame !

It is my happy privilege and duty to give cordial welcome to all who have gathered here, — to the officers and citizens of this town of Marshfield and this county of Plymouth in which Webster lived, and to my fellow-citizens of this Commonwealth of which he was so many years the admiration and glory. I welcome the Ancient and Honorable Artillery company and the veteran soldiers of the Grand Army, whose gunpowder was ground from Webster's logic. In the name of the Commonwealth and in behalf of the Webster Historical Society, I also cordially welcome the distinguished guests who have come from beyond our borders, the governors of our beloved sister New England States, and especially him whose name I have kept till last, in order to present him first, the President of the United States. Welcome, sir, to Massachusetts and to Marshfield, to the State of the Adamses, whose successor you are, and to the grave of Webster, but for whom it is hardly too much to say that to-day they would have no successor. Massachusetts thinks no courtesy too great, no greeting too cordial, to bestow upon the chief magistrate of the nation in which there is no stauncher or more loyal state. But with especial interest does she welcome you, remembering your association with Garfield, whom she honored and loved, the dignity with which you bore the terrible ordeal of his long agony of death and succeeded to his place, and the courage and force of conviction with which, on more than one occasion, you have exercised the prerogative of your great office. Fellow-citizens, I present to you the President of the United States.

MAYOR PRINCE.

I think, Mr. Mayor, you will agree with me — who
have so recently passed through the ordeal to which you
are now subjected — that it is on an occasion like this
far more blessed to give than to receive. And yet, next
to the pleasure which I feel in presenting to you this,
your portrait, — the cordial gift of many friends, —
must be that which you feel in the regard in which they
hold you, and of which it is only the expression. Nor is
it possible that you could deem any monument more en-
viable than this likeness of yourself, the citizen magistrate
of the modern Athens, hanging upon the walls of one of
her sacred temples of learning, forever in the presence of
the soulful faces and expanding intelligence of her children, who for generations hence will hither come to drink
at the fountains of intellectual life, to be inspired by noble
examples, and thus to lay the deep foundations of character. The schoolroom is the very garden of immortality.
Classes may come and classes may go, but there still flows
in forever the springtide of rosy youth. And, communi-
cating itself to your double here, from whom from this
day hence you part company in respect to growing old,
he, too, shall never know or feel the lapse of years, but
always be the polished scholar and gentleman he is to-
day. And when, as I trust may be the case, long after
the twentieth century shall have begun its round, you

will perchance enter again these doors, — your cane, no
doubt, in hand, just as the artist has given it to you here,
— it may be that some school-child will guide your steps
with her little hand, and, pointing thither, tell you, in
innocent ignorance of your identity, that it is the picture
of one of Boston's good old mayors, who for many years
presided over her destinies, who loved her for her ancient
fame and her later worth, who in many graceful orations
maintained her reputation for eloquence, who identified
himself with her progress in learning, art, and literature,
and who, fostering her schools, did not forget that the
education of all her children is her greatest duty and her
proudest achievement.   If the child shall assure you that
it was at the time of its suspension an excellent likeness,
she will tell you, though the flattering compliment may at
this moment somewhat severely test your modesty, only
the simple truth.   If ever an artist was to be congratu-
lated upon a success which leaves nothing to be desired,
and which has reproduced his subject to the very life, it
is Mr. Parker, in this effort of his skill.   There are those
who doubt the propriety of public portraits of the living;
but at least in your case, sir, I cannot believe the city will
suffer any detriment.   As for yourself, though you were
the best of men, you would be a better one remembering
that children at school look daily on your face ; and I am
sure you and I enjoy our portraits far more than if their
execution were postponed until after our own.   As for
your fellow citizens, why should they be debarred the
pleasure of thus exhibiting their regard for one whom
they have already paid the greater tribute of choosing so
many times to be the chief magistrate of their city?

Mr. Mayor, my duty is done.   It affords me great and
perhaps a vindictive pleasure to leave you, as you so re-

cently left me, to the painful embarrassment, from which, however, your facility will easily release you, of responding to the presentation of your own portrait, and of pronouncing an oration of which you shall yourself be the sole topic. Let me only add how cordially my own personal sympathies go with the words I have uttered in behalf of those of whom I am the representative in presenting this excellent likeness. I congratulate you, Mayor Prince, upon an honor now conferred upon you, greater than the laurel wreath, in that a plain Boston schoolhouse has this day been dedicated, to which your name has been given, and on the walls of which your picture hangs.

RESPONSE

BOTH as representing a Commonwealth made up in part of the Plymouth Colony, of which John Carver was the first governor, and personally as a resident of Plymouth County and a descendant from Pilgrim stock, it is with great pleasure that I join to-day in this commemoration of the landing of that band of exiles who, two hundred and sixty years ago, moored their bark on what we have, indeed, amid this morning's storm, found to be the wild New England shore. I am glad to pay them the tribute of Massachusetts, for, as the germ of the oak is in the acorn, the germ of our Commonwealth, alike in herself and as she represents the nation at large, was in the group which clustered that December day on Plymouth Rock.

In responding for her I speak for no class or calling, but for all her men and women. I rejoice that she is to-day — on a larger scale — just what the Pilgrim community was, more than two centuries and a half ago, — a community the virtue of which is not in its governors, or preachers, or captains, but in its homes and firesides, its families like those in the picture in Pilgrim Hall, and its plain men and women who live temperate, pure, and wholesome lives, who constitute the ranks of a stable citizenship, who go about their daily toil, who sustain our schools, and who are the foundations of society. It is

Miles Standish still who stands ready at call to shoulder his musket for the common defense. It is Elder Brewster still who pitches the popular sentiment, and discharges whatever public or private duty falls to his hands. It is Priscilla still who is the saint of the New England home, — sweetheart, wife, or mother.

Massachusetts has, perhaps, her faults ; but if so, they are of the surface. Her heart beats always true and sound. There is the ideal as well as the historic life in states as there is in men. Charles Lamb, looking at the epitaphs in a graveyard, asked where all the bad people were buried. It was wit ; it was not wisdom. There was not a record there that did not truly tell the ideal life, which was the only thing worth telling, and which, through whatever sin or folly, the poor heart that lay beneath had recognized and aspired to reach. And so of the Commonwealth, the question to be asked is, What is its ideal ? You know what it is. You recognize it by your coming here. You read it in the verse of Whittier. You read it in the blundering scrawl, in which the Massachusetts boy, writhing over his first composition, tries to express the aspiration he has drunk in from the very air. You read it in the unerring public sentiment to which there still lies an appeal from all artificial tribunals. It is not wealth ; it is not power ; it is not the survival of the fittest : it is the consecration of all to the happiness and freedom of each one ; it is the recognition of the value of a single human soul. Under such a test the glory of the Roman soldier, of Grecian art, of kingdoms and empires, fades away. The Pilgrim and the Puritan stand forth. John Carver and John Winthrop reach down and clasp the hands alike of John Andrew and of a hospital nurse. The fire gleams on a farmer's hearth, at which an eager-eyed boy reads a book. The son of a New England missionary devotes his life to the education of the shy and bruised Indian, as well as of the enfranchised slave, to deliver whom from bondage he had already risked his life in battle. The freemen of a town gather in a homely shed to raise money by taxation, and to discuss the laying out of a way. A mother kisses her son as he goes to fight for his country, and looks not on his face again until it cannot answer back her tears. A housewife, her table cleared, runs to visit the sick. There is no village in which are not the schoolroom, the library, the town house, and the church. Thrift and industry are indoors and out of doors; wealth and labor alike mean refinement and growth. And amid this scene he is greatest who is the servant of all.

It is all the enlarged expression of what was in the heart and faith of the Pilgrim. Across the years Massachusetts pays him her tribute of gratitude and love.

THE OLD SIXTH.

AT THE DINNER OF THE REGIMENTAL ASSOCIATION, AT LOWELL,
APRIL 19, 1881.

I KNOW I need not assure you, Mr. President, of my
sincere interest in the celebration of this anniversary.
Personally, I cannot forget that among the members of
the Sixth were not only those who were friends of mine
when I lived in this part of Middlesex County, but young
men to whom I was teacher and companion at the academy in Westford. And as the exercises in the square recall the memory of the first martyrs of the regiment, I
feel, too, a just pride that two of them were born in my
own native State. But far above all personal considera-
tions is the tender, thrilling, eternal interest which the
Commonwealth which I have the honor, at this time, to
represent, forever feels in every soldier, every name, every
event, that attaches to her Old Sixth regiment. It was
the first to march to the front; the first to spill its blood;
the first to throw around the national capital in its defense that living wall of patriotism which from that time
forward never was broken. Its name recalls the heart-
throb of Andrew, whose tender message, vibrating along
the electric wires, electrified at the same time the finer
wires of the soul of the whole republic, and whose noble
oration over the graves of Ladd and Whitney here in
your city's midst still echoes in your ears. It recalls, too,
the beginning of the brightest part of the career of that
distinguished citizen of Lowell, whose earnest political op-

ponent I have been and am, but whose patriotic, prompt, and incisive services in the war for union and liberty I never forget. And, finally, it links forever the nineteenth of April, 1775, and the nineteenth of April, 1861, — the villages and farms of Middlesex and the streets of Baltimore, — and has made it the reddest-letter day in the history of American independence and equal rights.

What an exquisite tribute it is to the immortality of the human soul, that what we call a great event is never in the event itself, but in the sentiment, the unseen, intangible, immortal idea for which the event stands! Prick my finger with a penknife, and the blood that flows from the wound cannot be distinguished from that which ran from the patriotic veins of Needham or Whitney. The ranks which marched that day through Baltimore are exactly, in material and character, like those of the Mechanic Phalanx, under whose graceful escort we have just paraded these peaceful streets. But the names of those martyrs and of the companies that stood at bay in the Monumental City are as eternal as the memory of Thermopylæ, while we are only the ephemeral motes of a sunbeam. Show to Agassiz but the fragments of a bone, and to his illumined intelligence the whole animal of which that bone was once a part stands forth complete. And so mention hereafter to the world the crimsoned church green at Lexington or the blood of the Sixth sprinkling the Baltimore pavements, and lo! there will lie outstretched the whole story of the Revolution, culminating in independence, and the whole story of the war of the Rebellion, culminating in universal liberty. They are the red milestones of history.

The words we use on these occasions are fervid. And yet how weak they are! The scene we now recall will never have its true grandeur till centuries hence shall give it a background and make it stand out like the glory of a cloud on the horizon at sunrise. Proud may you and your children be that you were actors in that scene. Memory, vivid as it is, can hardly restore it to you, — the intense patriotic rush of feeling at the north, — the electrifying call to arms, — the rallying at Boston, — the sympathies of friends, bursting from window and door and pavement, bidding you adieu and swearing an eternal gratitude, to which the Commonwealth has never been unfaithful, — the acclaim of city after city as you went on to the defense of the national capitol, — and the intense hour, twenty years ago this day, when you first met the mad torrent of treason, bore its insults and murder, and rolled it back forever. It was great because it was typical. It was freedom confronting slavery, — loyalty against treason, — the civilization of Massachusetts, the dignity of labor represented by her mechanics, the common school represented by her young heroes rushing from farm and desk and shop, against the barbarism of caste. Well may Middlesex County, well may these fair cities of Lowell and Lawrence, well may these clustering villages that contributed to that day, cherish with undying pride the memory of their heroes. For the Commonwealth I gladly bring her tears, her tributes, to mingle with your own, and I thank you for every pageant, every trumpet-blast, every drum-beat, every eloquent word with which you hand down for the education of her children these lessons of patriotism.

Mr. President, freshly impressed as I am with the peculiar relation of the Commonwealth to the Sixth, — the most dramatic and memorable of her regiments, — forgive me if I say, with what pride I should place in the executive chamber, where sat Andrew who gloried so in your glory, there to be kept, except as from time to time your regiment or its association desire them, these your colors, in the disposition of which my judgment has been invited. It is no mere question of ownership. They are the common glory of the Commonwealth. It was an acute lawyer — the meanest things are always attributed to the lawyers, Mr. President — who, when two fishermen disputed over an oyster, gave a half shell to each and kept the pearl that lay between for his own fee. I would follow his example and take these your pearls of great price, but not, like him, for myself. I would hang them where, henceforth, they will tell me and my successors, and legislature after legislature, and the whole people, the story of the gallant Sixth, — the story of the mechanics and farmers who showed what is this American people who are at once citizens and soldiers, and who know not only how to make and conduct a government, but how to defend it. Let them tell the story of the tragic march through Baltimore, — the story of the martyrdom of Taylor, Needham, Ladd, and Whitney, and of the services of those other still living heroes whom I forbear to name lest I omit any. And when, in some future crisis, Massachusetts again calls to arms let her sons look up to them and feel their blood tingle to be worthy to rank with the heroes of 1861, as you, twenty years ago this day, proved yourselves worthy, in the judgment of your countrymen and of history, to rank with the heroes of 1775.

ADDRESS

AT THE DEDICATION OF OAKES AMES MEMORIAL BUILDING,
EASTON, MASS., NOVEMBER 17, 1881.

WHAT a tender New England feeling is in the legend, engraved in letters of stone, which met our eyes as we entered these doors : " This building was erected in memory of Oakes Ames by his children." One hardly knows whether such a splendid edifice reflects more credit upon the father to whose memory and in honor of whose great enterprise and public spirit it has been reared, or upon the sons who have exhibited such generous measure of filial love and piety.

Oakes Ames sat in the council of John A. Andrew and helped him fight the good fight for freedom. Transferred to the national councils, it was the power of his will and genius that conquered the snows and peaks of the Rocky Mountains, and put an iron girdle round about the American continent in forty minutes. It was a gigantic work which hardly any other hand was strong enough to undertake, and to which to-day no man who knew him doubts that he brought also the patriotic purpose of binding closer the Union, the peril of which he had just seen, and of putting it still more rapidly forward on the road of its mighty development. Here, too, at home behold memorials of his benevolence which stand all around us in this his native town, bequeathed by him to his sons in that spirit of enterprise which is their richest and best inheritance, and consummated by them in these comfortable homes of labor.

What a compendium of American history is such a wondrous American life! The early struggles; the common-school education; the apprenticeship to an humble trade; the blacksmith's swinging arm; the best pride of New England blood and ancestry; the institution of special lines of manufacture and art; their steady enlargement; the outgrowth then of larger purposes; the growing interest in the public weal and progress; the respect won from fellow-citizens; the elevation to high place and opportunity; the ultimate conquering of fortune; and the crowning achievement of success and a name! It is a tribute, as are this occasion and building, not to American wealth, but to American worth and American growth.

Yet let me turn again and congratulate the sons who, mindful at once of good taste and utility, have paid this tribute of their filial affection and gratitude to the father whom none could know as they knew him, and whose heart, if ever the sorrows which fall on all weighed it down, found life worth living in their love and in a loyalty, which, surviving the grave, holds no trust so sacred as the honor of his name. The father's memory, — the memory of him who, remembering his own boyhood, determined that ours should lack no help that he could give it; who stood to our youth the very soul of honor and nobility; who led us by the hand; who taught us our first lessons; whose heart, as now so well we know, yearned toward us with so much hope and pride and longing; the greeting smile of whose face and the clasp of whose hand come back to us in dreams; and whom death even takes not from us, but only the more clearly reveals to us as the truest friend we ever knew! — we each of us erect to our father's memory our monument, though not like this. With most of us it is a modest headstone, and the green

turf wet with our tears.   But we can all share in the feelings that have given birth to this magnificent memorial, —
not a cumbrous and curious obelisk fantastically cut with
characters that time shall shatter and future ages be unable to decipher ; not a cold, forbidding mausoleum, suggestive of death and decay, and rotting into the earth, —
not a monumental arch to which the idle creeping ivy
clings, and through which howl the barren winds, but a
great hall warm with life and activity, for the meeting
of townsmen and free citizens, where the public interest,
which so stirred the heart of Oakes Ames, shall have
voice; where the welfare of the people shall be promoted ;
where thrifty industry shall send its representatives ;
where refining amusements shall delight them ; where
orators shall speak, and song and music swell ; and where
he shall still live for years to come in the hearts of the
people of this town, and in the larger and more enlightened life to which his works so largely contributed.

LONGFELLOW.

At Unitarian Church, East Boston, April 2, 1882.

It was a delightful thought to devote the April softness of this Sunday afternoon, this best day of our cheerful and sunny religion, to Longfellow, — to the companionship of a gentle poet, and to the influence of a spirit which now, and for time to come, will mellow our sadnesses with tender hymns of resignation, will inspire us far up the heights with his song, and will fill our lives, though we grow to be bent and gray, with children's hours. We are here to sing with him, not to mourn him. Why is it that we used to shudder at this death, which now we find only strings the chords of a more comprehending love, and opens full to view the sweetness and light which the dust of life half hid before? Have you not looked at a picture, and only been blinded by the sunbeam that shot across it? It was not till the sunbeam went out that the lineaments stood forth relieved and distinct. What a poor and meagre chain of little-meaning links is this narrative of dates and events which we sometimes call a man's life! It is of little consequence, except for the dear association's sake, what was the name or residence or birthplace or age of the poet. Of what interest to us is even the great globe of the sun in itself, compared with the radiance which is its soul and which fills the universe with light! Do not tell me that Longfellow was born, and had honors and degrees and a professorship, and crossed the seas; for these things come and go, and now flash, now faint. But tell me that his mind was full of gentle and ennobling thoughts, for these live forever. Tell me that he loved children, and wrote songs for them and of them ; and let me hear my little girl, as she comes down the happy morning stairway, repeat untaught the verses which he made, and which are a bridge from his soul to hers, and from all human souls to one another. The material is nothing, and dies ; but the soul sings on, and, in these tributes which we and many another assembly are paying it, we are asserting and proving its immortality. When some poor creature, with nothing but a throne and a crown, dies, his subjects hail his successor, and shout, *The king is dead, long live the king !* When our king, the poet, is laid to rest, we may well cry, *The poet is dead, long live the poet !* For he succeeds himself, and is dead only to live, even on earth, a larger and more present life in his verse, and in the songs and hearts of the people.

It is a poor commonplace to say that Longfellow is the poet of the people, for no poet is a great or true poet who is not that. And what a tribute is this to our common humanity ! Lives of great men all remind us not so much that we can make our lives sublime, as that our lives are sublime, if only we will not cumber or debase them. Not by putting into melody something that is beyond and above you and me, not by breathing a music so strained that it never trembles in our fancies and prayers, does the poet rise to excellence, but by voicing the affections, the finer purpose, the noblenesses, that are in the great common nature, — in the sailor up the shrouds, in the maiden lashed to the floating mast, in the mother laying away her child, in the schoolboy at his task or play, or counting the sparks that fly from the blacksmith's forge, in the man at

his work or, when he rests from it, raided by blue-eyed
banditti from the stairway and the hall.   So the poet
teaches us not our disparity from him but our level with
him ; not our meanness, but our loftiness.   Let us not
forget that he owes as much to those who inspire him to
sing their thoughts, as they to him for singing them.   The
music he wrote is all lying unwritten in us.   Let us sing
it in our lives, which we can, as he sung it from his pen,
which we cannot.

It was a beautiful life.   It was felicitous beyond ordinary lot.   The birds sang in its branches.   The sun shone
and the April showers fell softly upon it.   And, while he
now slumbers, let us read his verse anew.   With his
hymns in our ears, may we, like him, leave behind us foot-
prints in the sands of time ; may our sadness resemble
sorrow only as the mist resembles the rain ; may we know
how sublime a thing it is to suffer and be strong ; may we
wake the better soul that slumbered to a holy, calm delight ; may we never mistake heaven's distant lamps for
sad, funereal tapers ; and may we ever hear the voice from
the sky like a falling star, — Excelsior !

ADDRESS

AT THE CELEBRATION OF THE TWO HUNDREDTH ANNIVERSARY
OF THE BUILDING OF THE OLD MEETING-HOUSE AT HINGHAM,
MASS., AUGUST 8, 1881.

IT was to be presumed, as indeed the event has shown, that nothing due to the anniversary we celebrate, whether of tender memories, of grateful tribute, of lesson from the past or suggestion for the future, would be left unsaid by an orator [Charles Eliot Norton] so fitting to the occasion alike in himself and in his descent from the first minister who preached within these walls. Yet, even as when we honor some man distinguished for nobility of life, or greatness of achievement, or the ripe and venerated perfection of age, we crowd around him to add to our spokesman's word our own loving salutation or even the mute pressure of the hand; so to-day, though we but repeat the thoughts already better spoken, we throng this ancient shrine, we venerate these ancient walls, we reach through the centuries to grasp the hand of Peter Hobart or John Norton and from full hearts we cannot but speak our word of gratitude and affection. In such a spirit we stand here no longer as we should stand in any other house. I look not alone upon the scene that fills the outward eye. These pews, these faces, these costumes, disappear, and in place of all this the unceiled rafters are over my head; no paint discolors the wood; the rude carving of the axe is the only decoration; oaken, unbacked benches fill the floor, the women on one side, the men on the other; the musket leans against the knee; and the stern face of the English Puritan, clad in the garb of his day, a subject of King Charles, yet never a slave to him or to the forms of his church, looks back upon my gaze.

As a member of this parish, though of a branch of it springing from the same deep root, — as a citizen of this ancient town, which in its municipal capacity, and at the common charge, bought this land and built this house, and for aught I know still owns it, at least so far as to be entitled to share in its preservation and honor, and which for more than a hundred years here had its town-meetings and discussed great themes of public right and safety and of civil liberty, — and, finally, as a representative of the Commonwealth which counts in all its borders no church edifice so old and so sacred as this, I come to lay my gift upon its altar, and to pay my tribute to the men who raised its frame, to the men who have handed it down as a sacred trust, and to the men in whose loyal keeping it is to-day. Indeed it is not unfitting that the Commonwealth should have a special interest in this building; for, when in 1681 a difference of opinion arose as to where it should be set, as such differences sometimes have arisen in the best regulated New England religious societies, it was the governor who, with unhesitating disregard of the wishes of the parish, took the matter into his own hands and ordered the house to be set on the spot where it now stands. And as everybody is to-day content with that and would regard any suggestion of a change as sacrilege, it is a significant illustration of how superior is the judgment of a governor to that of all others, and how much better he can direct the affairs of people than they can themselves. Alas! I fear his authority has since then been greatly impaired, and if he were now to interfere with the slightest detail of parish administration, his occupation would soon be gone.

The nineteenth century will not again see such an anniversary as this, — the celebration of the two hundredth anniversary of the raising of a Puritan meeting-house, — no other so old still used for Protestant public worship in the United States. Of the five successive ministers who have preached from its pulpit, the last still lives, and is to-day the sole pastor of its congregation. Still more remarkable is the fact that, during the two hundred and fifty years' existence of the parish, six ministers span the whole period. And may not such a parish, yes, may not this town, may not Massachusetts, turn with pride to the list. One a graduate from Magdalen College, Cambridge, four from Harvard, and one from Dartmouth. Peter Hobart, the Sam Adams of the colony, known as an apostle of civil liberty even more than as a preacher of the gospel; John Norton, who exemplified and taught the Christian life, and bore a name honored from that day to this in the church and in letters; Ebenezer Gay, who sounded the evangel of that more liberal faith which found its highest expression in Channing and its fruit in the absolute religious freedom of to-day; Henry Ware, another revered Unitarian name, suggestive of the refinement of learning and the culture of college halls; Joseph Richardson, who, preceding John Quincy Adams in Congress, thus reunited church and state; Calvin Lincoln, the beloved friend and neighbor of us all, as saintly in his life as in his face, whom God has spared to enjoy this day, and whom may He yet spare for many years to enjoy the unbounded respect and love of all, irrespective of church or creed, who know him; and with these, also, Edward Horton, who has transferred the promise of his brilliant talents from this to a larger but not a better field! Well may Massachusetts hold in high and sacred esteem a church which through such men as Peter Hobart and his successors has, in the spirit of the highest independence, made its deep mark upon the tablets of civil liberty and religious thought. In that spirit of independence I find the seeds of our patriotic and free-thinking people and Commonwealth. In that I find, also, the cause of the separation — a separation that to-day exists only in tradition and name, and no longer in the hearts of either people — which led to the formation of the society of which the venerable Dr. Henry A. Miles is now the honored head. In that spirit of independence, too, I find the seeds of the paradox of that toleration, blooming out from the most uncompromising intolerance, which has since made this land an asylum for mankind, not alone for all classes of men, but for all shades of opinion, — also of that free inquiry which has laid the whole world, the world of matter and of soul, open to the touch of science and philosophy, — of that education which has made the dream of equality a homely fact, — of that politics which has made ours indeed a government of all the people. Were it mine to speak at length to-day, my theme should be the relation of this ancient meeting-house to civil government and civil liberty, which have here always gone hand in hand with the worship of God whose liberty maketh free, and in behalf of which this parish has sent its sons to their country's defense alike in the war for independence and the war for union and freedom, — and not only to the field, but also to the councils of the Commonwealth and of the republic. I would speak of it as a school and academy of training for the duties of the citizen, the wholesomeness of social life, the integrity of town and state.

And is not this typified in the very environments that surround us this midsummer day, — this happy, prosperous, enlightened community of Christian homes, this activity of life and growth where once the quiet of the forest slept? Yes, and this clustering and beautiful burying-ground, where death loses its terrors in the softness of repose beneath the leaves, and where now sleep not only the first settlers of Hingham, but the good and great and true who came after them, — the early pastors of this church, — the Thaxters of provincial fame in civil and military life, — that revolutionary hero, General Lincoln, who received Cornwallis's sword at Yorktown, — and John Andrew, that governor so dear to Massachusetts that only his name can be spoken, but never expression given to the love she bore him, — all these a part of the spirit of the thing we commemorate, and so all one with this parish and these hallowed walls. Can we take in all this, and all that the day recalls, and puts us in harmony with for two hundred and fifty years, and not rise to higher levels of feeling and of purpose? In 1869 the pastor of this society, Rev. Mr. Lincoln, said: "Only twelve years are wanting to complete two centuries since our fathers first assembled for Christian worship beneath this roof." Lo! the circle is rounded and the centuries are full. It shall be but a span and some one will say, "Only twelve years are wanting to complete three centuries." And, almost as soon, the finger of time will point their fulfillment, also. What shall they say of us? I trust it will be a word, — as ours is to-day, not of reproach but of honor, — of a church still inspiring an enlightened and fearless faith and a pure life, — of a town still loyal to good morals and advanced education, — of a Commonwealth still fortunate in the happiness, the intelligence, the progress of its people. Surely may these walls then still rise; this roof still echo back the voice of the preacher and choir; these rough-hewn timbers still be wreathed with the memory-wreaths of 1681, 1781, 1881. Mr. Solomon Lincoln, a distinguished son of Hingham and her historian, loyal to her honor and to this her chiefest pride, is with us to-day, no one with a finer enthusiasm, not in person but in spirit and in the presence of his sons who have so admirably taken part in the exercises of the occasion. May I not, in tribute to him and in expression of all our hearts, quote the words he put upon the parish seal, and say that, whether the third century shall be fulfilled, or the fourth, or the tenth, LET THE WORK OF OUR FATHERS STAND.

ADDRESS

At the Dedication of Town Hall, Hopedale, Mass., October 25, 1887.

THE substantial, yet modest, building which we have gathered to dedicate to the use of the people of this town marks the civilization of our time and commonwealth as exactly as a clock tells the hour. It is one of the accurate measures by which the genius of history will gauge the moral and material status of this generation, the present condition of capital and labor in Massachusetts, the tendency of the creep of the overflow of wealth, the participation of the masses in the good things of the flesh and the spirit, the elevation reached in the thermometer of popular esthetics and ideals, and the conscious obligation of abundance to minister to common human progress. The impulse that gave it birth has its roots in something deeper and remoter than any personal benefactor, any family group of sons of Israel however generous, or any distinctive sentiment of a single community. It is the necessary and inevitable evolution, the natural flower of the seed of the human soul when given opportunity to spring to the light and develop its own capacity for beneficence.

Could there be a more striking contrast with the mighty edifices of ancient time than this modest building, not large enough to seat five hundred people! Yet the contrast is all in its favor. No happy labor, no freeman's cheerful song, no blessed thought of earning and saving for wife and children at home, went into their foundations or made them the artisan's hall for the exchange of his toil and skill for an equal share in all the blessings of his time. Here not a stone or brick or joint that was not fitted by an American citizen. No secret springs open its doors. No long and darkened corridors lead to its inner chambers. No rotting mummy is to hide in it for five thousand years. No helmeted figure towering seventy feet into the air, and armed with shield and spear, suggests an age of superstition and of war. No arena under its balconies reeks with ancient stain of blood and slaughter. But the democracy of a New England town gather in it in the exercise of self-government. Its walls echo with the debate of freemen. Its consecration is to temperance, the arts of peace, village improvement, and the interests of a simple, social, neighborhood life.

It represents three things in New England life. First, the accumulation of wealth, not by an individual but by a community, and indicative not of one rich man's prosperity, but of the common prosperity. It is an example of good socialism. On this spot, some forty years ago, one of those communities, which spring up from time to time, and of which so much is anticipated by the enthusiasm of their members, had undertaken, under the sweet guidance of the venerable and beloved Christian pastor who is here to-day, to solve the problem of a happy, industrious, and peaceful Christian brotherhood. It was a joint-stock association, sharing capital and profits, and run on common account. The result was a practical bankruptcy, averted only by a change which followed no longer any transcendental line, but turned to the line of hard, practical American business. For George Draper took the plant into his vigorous hand. An enlightened

and liberal selfishness became, as it usually does, a beneficence to which a weak communism was as the dull and
cheerless gleam of decaying punk to the inspiring blaze of
the morning sun in spring time. The man of affairs was
in temporal things a better leader than the priest, as he
usually is, and as nobody will so emphatically assure you
as the priest himself. A meagre manufacturing enterprise that made a few boxes and cotton-spinning temples
and employed a dozen hands, began that marvelous expansion which in these few years, under George Draper's
direction, has come to employ five hundred men; has
grown from an annual product of twenty thousand dollars
to one of more than twelve hundred thousand dollars;
has built and incorporated a Massachusetts town; has
erected these trim, convenient houses and homes of skilled
and prosperous labor; has enlarged the original enterprise into four great business houses, and embraces one
of the largest cotton machinery manufacturing centres in
the world.

In the second place this building stands for the New
England town-meeting. It thereby embodies the genius
of American political institutions. If there be anything
marked in the personal history of our American names,
it is the independence of their success and career from
all the ordinary props of what is supposed to be advanta-
geous individual fortune. What aid were they to Abraham Lincoln, Ben Franklin, Henry Clay, Horace Greeley,
Henry Wilson! It is upon the unmonopolized opportunities of American life that the citizen only need rely,
laying hold of those nearest at his hand to lift himself to
the upper air. Here some of the best of them will be in
especial readiness at his command. Ours is more and
more becoming a government of public opinion, and of

public opinion cumulated out of independent individual research, digestion, and debate. The accidental man in place is very much the involuntary agent of the public sentiment he represents — if a right man, the expression and agent of the best leadings of that sentiment; if a wrong man, then of its hesitations and obliquities. More and more the Town Hall, or whatever the theatre of public utterance, should tend to the making of the right man and the elimination of the wrong one, for more and more, in fact as well as in person, the citizen is becoming the sovereign. And his sovereignty, under whatever guise of democratic forms, will be a terrific despotism, if he be not a patriot rather than a demagogue, a representative rather of the schoolhouse than the grog-shop.

Undoubtedly there is in the near future that danger, which, like a weed springing out of the very luxuriance of fertility, springs from the very abundance of our prosperity and freedom. It is the danger which a writer in a recent review calls " a new fire deluge of barbarism, bursting out this time not from the outlying forests of the north, but from the volcano of human passions underneath our feet." The anarchist is already crying that the constitutional rule of the majority is as despotic as the tyranny of a czar. Against that danger the forces which this building represents and which it will concentrate will be a bulwark. That bulwark must be found in a condition of society which, on the one hand, extends to all a participation in its government, and on the other, gives all an access to its blessings, and thereby secures the corresponding responsibility that goes with the administration of the one and the enjoyment of the other. It must be found in a harmony of the conservative safeguards of property, institutions, law, and order with the flexible forces of progress. In other words, the function of this hall is to be a part of the Christian Church, as I doubt not it is intended to be, not in any ecclesiastical sense, but in the length and breadth of Christian civilization.

In the third place, this hall commemorates a noble New England life. George Draper deserves this strong and simple memorial. He was a strong, simple, massive character. There was granite in his foundations, and on it he erected a plain, substantial, and useful life. There was in him, as in this edifice, no attempt at useful ornamentation; but there were also no poor timbers. Everything was sound and square. He had that vigor of mind and purpose which commanded confidence and respect. You would not say he was a great man, as history applies that word to the exceptional few. And yet he was a great man, as one of that master class who dominate by force of purpose and persistence in achievement, and who lead, not because they point the way, but because, putting their broad shoulders to the tug, they draw a whole community along onward. In religion, a liberal Christian; in temperance, a total abstinent and prohibitionist; in politics, a Republican; he had much of that quality of the Puritan which is still left in New England, and which, flowering out into the larger liberality of our day, has been illustrated by so many men whose faces, long familiar to us, have recently passed away. There is always satisfaction, a sort of poetic fulfillment, when men, combining brain and will, start, develop, and achieve material enterprises, master material forces, and accumulate material wealth as a sign of their might. Such was George Draper, as all who knew him bear witness. He was, indeed, the architect of his own fortunes. His business grasp was comprehensive. He did not sit in a tub, but ranged the broad domain of productive industry, and saw its larger relations. He dealt with enlarging results, and could be in no community and not set in motion the wheels of enterprise, manufacture, product. Where he was, there the massed mill-stream turned the wheel, and the artisan's hammer rang.

Born in 1817, the son of an inventor, he added to his father's inventive genius the persistence that saw the invention wrought out to its complete result and profitable application to the processes of manufacture. A boy of fourteen, he worked in a cotton mill, and learned the principles of textile manufacturing. Three years later, relying on his own individual energies, industry, and pluck, and not on shibboleths, he rose to overseership. He served two years as a designer. He became superintendent of the great Otis Mills. And he had meantime acquired what Richard Cobden advised the working classes of England would make them free of the labor market of the world, to wit, an accumulation of twenty pounds, for he had saved, not one hundred, but five thousand dollars from his earnings. This was the cash capital he brought to Hopedale, in 1853, thirty-six years old. But inestimably greater was the capital he brought of character, energy, skill, and an inventive genius, which created forty or fifty patents of his own, and put into operation three or four hundred. I have already referred to the change he wrought in this community, inspiring life out of death. It was a splendid achievement of growth. It is a poetic miniature of the growth of that great country of which he was so true a patriot, and of which, in his life struggle, he was one of the staunchest upholders, giving of his means to its cause, and to its military service his son, now

the head of his house, whom it was his happiness to welcome back from the battlefield, not on, but with, his
shield. He was not of those who regarded his country
as an orange, to be squeezed. He stood by it in peace as
well as in war. He knew that it was no cold abstraction
for philosophers and theorists to dissect and diagnose, but
a great family of living human souls, of men and women
and children to be made happy and temperate and wise,
clothed with the comforts of life and blessed with the
refinements of homes. He knew that its foundation was
labor, the manual toil from which his own fortune sprang,
and back to which they still more and more contributed
as they grew. It was from his own experience in the hard
school of a laboring man, and from his later practical observation of the whole career of American industrial progress that he was for protecting his country in its labor and
industries so that the wages of the one and the prosperity
of the other should have every advantage legislation could
give them. He was a protectionist, because he believed
he had seen the withdrawal of protection followed by
hardship to labor and defeat to manufacturing enterprise,
and its return restoring both to prosperity. It was not a
matter of theory with him, but of practical business adjustment, just as it was in England with Cobden, who,
had he lived in the United States, would have advocated
the same policy, because they both sought the same end,
— the encouragement of home manufactures, — and, as
practical men, took the directest path to it which the peculiar circumstances of each country suggested.

To that policy of protection, with honest conviction,
George Draper gave allegiance. He contributed largely
and effectively to its literature and argument. His letters
in the newspapers, his terse pamphlets, are familiar as

household words. Of the cause of temperance he was, by
precept, by example, by helping hand and purse, a life-
long and earnest advocate and pusher. But his best contributions are in this village around us. Go forth. and
look upon the scene. Behold the farms redeemed, the
sterile and rocky acres turned to fair fields, the two poor
shops of thirty years ago replaced by twenty solid and
capacious buildings, all alive with intelligent labor, and
with machinery that seems almost intelligent, the product,
largely, of his own genius. Behold a population sex-
tupled in numbers and in possessions, all drawn from this
plant. Could he speak, he would ask you, as you look,
what man has he, the protected protectionist, robbed? At
whose expense, and by despoiling whom, has he wrought
this result? What farmer of the West, or anywhere, has
he robbed by creating this new market for the farmer's
produce? What element of labor has he robbed by furnishing it this variety of employment here and elsewhere,
and enabling it not only to support itself, but to lay by
savings? What Southern planter and freedman has he
robbed by inventing swifter means of buying and con-
suming their cotton crop? What consumer the broad
land over has he subjected to a robber's tribute by so
developing his mechanical inventions that he has increased
the supply, improved the make, and reduced the price of
textile fabrics everywhere and for everybody?

On the 9th of June last this village was still. Its mills
were closed, its labors suspended. For its people were
laying the body of George Draper to rest beneath the
turf. Not gloomily, for was it not the poetic fulfillment
of a fortunate life? Great statesmen have lived to see
no face brighten at their coming, or died counting all
their honors lost because some later honor was not won.

But when his soul went up, it may well have cast back a look of calm satisfaction on the work he had done, — complete, because still in progress; happy groups of families and homes; the fading sunlight falling on church spires and schoolroom windows; the air tremulous with the hum of happy and prosperous labor; behind him the godspeed of grateful hearts, before him the "well done." To-day, again the mills of Hopedale rest, but for a sunny purpose. In keeping with his expressed purpose, his children have erected, for the free use of his townsmen, this Town Hall. We now dedicate it to his memory, and to the use of the people among whom and for whom he lived; whose happiness and welfare is his best tribute; and of whom in his career of toil and triumph, of whom in his simplicity of manner and living, of whom in his temperance, industry, and integrity, of whom in all that makes for honored American citizenship, he was so genuinely and exemplarily one.

JAMES A. GARFIELD.

At Williams College Commencement, July 6, 1881.

The days that cluster around our glorious Fourth, turning its glory into sadness, are days not of alarm but sorrow. The heart of the nation is broken and melts in tears, but its faith and courage are unshaken. For the second time in the history of our republic a president has been shot by an assassin. But this time, thank God, no organized political or social purpose or significance crouches close behind the deed. The great victim lies not a sacrifice to partisan or sectional malignity. The party of half the people whose gallant candidate he defeated; the belt of humbled states which stood solid against his election, as they stood solid less than twenty years ago against his sword, and even the embittered malcontents in his own ranks had no hand in his murder. But all alike, in the better nobility of human nature, now stand in common horror and pity over his wounds. Nay, the whole world, betraying its genuine faith and hope in the American Republic, lifts its outstretched arms, and its hands are filled with the lilies of sympathy for us and for him. No decree, issued through the secret channels of banded socialists, made his assailant their slave and tool. The czar fell beneath the avenging and relentless pursuit of organized murder. Abraham Lincoln fell the last and noblest martyr of a civil war which, victorious upon the field, yet carried in its train the forked and hissing flames of treachery and assassination. But Garfield, in a time of profound peace, when, aided by his own generous words, the sympathies of the Union were welding into their old fraternity ; in a time of universal prosperity, when the whole land smiles with the promise of plenteous harvests ; in a country the very atmosphere of which is freedom, — Garfield, the embodiment of American humanity ; whose name a year ago was on these walls as the hope and example not only of the scholar, but of the poor and humble ; upon whom the only criticism was upon the boyish and bubbling sympathy of his nature ; who had risked his life in battle for his fellow men, and pitched his voice in peace to the highest notes of liberty, — Garfield falls bleeding beneath the crazy pistol-shot of a fool. The monstrous meaninglessness of the purpose robs the deed of its horror. But not meaningless is its lesson. If the will that did the killing was that of a maniac, yet the maniac takes his cue as well as other men. This time, so far as he took it from the nihilist's sophistry and the spectacle of the czar's death, let it be a warning. So far as he took it from the poisonous example of great party leaders dragging the honor of American politics into the mire of spoils and plunder, let it be a warning. So far as he took it from a system which makes the holding of civil office the reward of the most persistent camp-follower and go-between, let it be a warning. These are lessons which this awful calamity teaches. But it does not shake the foundations of that " government of the people which shall not perish from the earth." If the murderer was of sound mind, let his punishment be stern, swift, and sure. If not, or in any event, terrible as is the blow, it is like the lightning, which knows no respect of persons, save that the tallest monarch of the forest oftenest attracts and takes the stroke. Let no worshiper of more absolute government find in this event a charge against our own. In the prophetic and reverent words of the president himself upon the death of Lincoln, " God reigns, and the government at Washington still lives."

When the rumor came, as it came at first, that Garfield was dead, we recalled not more the president than the man. It is one of our own number that has been stricken down. It is the poor boy of our own youth, bare of foot and weighted with poverty, lifting his eyes through humble toil to the heights of American education and opportunity. It is our own classmate, revisiting the college halls and classic scenes of his youth to lay the wreath of his great glory at the feet of his Alma Mater, and to read in the loving eyes of his wife and children the honest pride that comes from the hand-clasp and congratulations of those who knew and loved him in early days. It is the comrade of our own veterans, who fought with him at Chickamauga. It is our own tribune, who, on the floor of Congress, upon the platform in many a brave and inspiring word to his countrymen, young and old, has spoken so nobly for humanity, for equal rights, for honest money, for high ideals and systems of political service, and for the national advancement. And it is to the wife and mother, not of the president, but of one of our own number, that our tenderest sympathies go forth as we recall the ripe and bending years of the one whose brow is still happy with the inauguration kiss of her boy, and whose life spans at once the Western pioneer's cabin and the White House, — a tragedy at either end, — or recall the other from school days till now, who has alike brightened his simple Western home, and to-day, watching at his bedside, stands for the heroism of American womanhood. In sympathy with them both I offer the prayer which is breathed by the whole Commonwealth, from Greylock's top to the pebbles upon the beach at Provincetown, — a prayer for the restoration to health and post, and for the return another year to these beautiful scenes with which his name and memory will be forever associated, of Williams' foremost graduate, Massachusetts' distinguished descendant, and the nation's beloved president, James A. Garfield !

ADDRESS

This is certainly a great day for Cape Cod. The spirit of celebration is echoing all along its sandy length and illuminating the waters that lovingly embrace it on either side. On the first day of last month we reëmbalmed the Pilgrims who made this shore the stepping-stone to the Plymouth threshold, and round whom, as their shattered bark came in from the perils of the deep, the Cape threw its great protecting arm. To-day we again honor the Pilgrim and pay our tribute to the fathers who planted and the sons who have watered the good seed which, under the blessing of God, has had this great increase.

A few months ago we celebrated the centennial of the inauguration of our National Government. And yet what we were celebrating as a beginning was itself an accomplished work, resulting not from any special cause or particular event, but from the natural growth and development of a political and social system which had started at Plymouth and Boston and here in Sandwich a century and a half earlier. It was a system under which brave and intelligent Christian freemen, settling our coast and expanding toward the interior, lived in simple ways, pursued homely avocations, tilled the soil, built vessels, engaged in commerce, combined hard manual labor with good social position, enjoyed a democratic church, brought education to the threshold of every child, inaugurated a republican form of government by representation, and prepared the popular mind by a thorough training of a hundred and fifty years for the responsibilities which national independence brought. Thus it was that what seemed to Europe the miraculous spectacle of a people suddenly assuming self-government and a constitution of equal rights, was really no stranger than that the oak, strong with the growth of centuries, should endure the tempest which sways its leafy top, but disturbs not its trunk or its roots. The institution of the New England town was the college where these students in local self-government graduated, and every man in New England was such a student. As I think of their work, the consummation of which we celebrate to-day, and the story of which the orator of the morning has rehearsed, I look back through the long vista of years with a feeling of profound respect and veneration. You could, to-day, in other lands have visited shrines of grander fame, over which are temples wrought by masters of architecture, and gorgeous with the work of masters of art. You could, in imagination, re-create from Greek and Roman and still more Oriental ruins the magnificent grandeur and glory of dynasties that have ruled the world. You could, in Westminster Abbey, hold communion with illustrious dead who won the most conspicuous glory of warrior and statesman, orator, poet, scholar, and divine. But none of these suggest to us the humanity and beauty and significance of the birthplace of a town like this. For here no broken column of fallen temples tells of the magnificence and luxury of the few wrung from the poverty and degradation of the many ; no statue or shrine perpetuates not so much the greatness of one man as the inferiority of the body of the people. Here rather began that growth of a free people, that common recognition in town organization of the equal rights of all men, which could not endure that any child should be uneducated; or that any poor should remain unfed; or that any one caste should hold supremacy and another be ground under foot; or that any slave should long breathe Massachusetts air. The civilization of other peoples has been a slow evolution from misty and barbarous beginnings, aided even by the invasion or conquest of other powers. Our fathers began at the summit, standing clear and self-sustained against the sunrise. There are no shadowy beginnings, no day of mean things; no semi-barbarism, out of which there has been an exodus, but rather always a spirit of advanced intellectual and national life. No more generous enthusiasm for learning goes into your schools' to-day than they put into theirs. They dotted your landscape with the spires of churches. I love these towns, and sigh that for more than half the people of the Commonwealth they exist no longer. Think what magnificent memories and associations they embody for us, and how crowded is the record of every one of them with heroic names and with participation in great heroic events. We are no longer the new world. We are venerable with age. Progress moves now so swift that a hundred years are more than a thousand in the middle ages. We look back through the vista of two centuries and a half and it is filled with great achievements in behalf of humanity; with great names of heroic men and women who lived not afar off, but were with us and of us; and with such great events as the success of popular government, the emancipation of human thought and faith, the abolition of slavery, and the inventions of science, which have put the globe into the hollow of man's hand and made the giant powers of nature obedient servants of human will. They will some day scoop out the Cape Cod Ship Canal as deftly as a lady dips a spoon. With what ancestry in the world shall we fear to compare ours? Our soil is rich with the ashes of the good and great, and our tribute goes out to them the more warmly because it goes not to the few; not to an illustrious warrior here or a great benefactor there; but to the whole body of those plain, God-fearing and self-respecting men and women who so raised the general level of their ordinary life that any distinction among them which they made was the accident of circumstance or necessity, and any distinction which we should make would be an injustice. What trust have they not imposed upon us? With them behind us, what is not our duty as the living, accountable citizens of this and other like communities to-day to those who shall follow us? Shall we lower the standard? Shall we not rather advance it still higher? The world is pleading with us from our safe and high vantage ground to lend a helping hand to reach down to our fellow men and lift them up by help and by example. There never was a time when the moral instincts were more sensitive than now. Peace spreads her white wings over us. There is indeed no field on which to battle with bloody arms for civil freedom, for religious toleration, or against beast or savage foe. Our conflict must be with the insidious forces that war upon the moral sentiment, that threaten corruption to our social and political fabric, that invade the manhood and purity and truth of men, that impair the sanctity and happiness of home, or that would subvert the institutions that have made New England a paradise of living, as it is a paradise of varied and invigorating climate, scenery, and seashore. The obligations of the noble record along which you look back for two hundred and fifty years with so much pride, are not to seek for great opportunities remote and afar off, but to aid in the circle of our own immediate influence and ability in upbuilding the citizen; in eradicating the subtle evil of intemperance that is honeycombing society and the state with its rot; in diffusing the common education of the people, for which the fathers provided so sedulously; in adjusting not so much the cold, economic relation of capital and labor, as if these were distinct factors, but the warm relation of man with man in the great struggle for happiness, in which every man is a capitalist and every man a laborer; and in standing firm against any influence or inroad that threatens the purity of democratic government. The civilization of the future is in our own hands. These great causes of temperance, of the education of the masses, of the purity of our politics, depend upon our discharge or neglect of our duty. If we discharge it, then are we worthy sons of worthy sires. If we neglect it, then is our celebration of these anniversaries, our praise of the fathers, our tributes to their virtues, but sounding brass and tinkling cymbal.

ADDRESS

On the Spirit of 1775, at the Centennial Tea Party, at Agricultural Hall, Hingham, Mass., August 12, 1875.

WE seek to revive to-night, my friends, something of the spirit and circumstance of 1775. You will remember that, only a hundred years ago, our fatherland — now magnificent in extent and wealth, with navies and a militia of millions at its command, with systems of education, industry, and growth that give it foremost rank among the nations — was but a slender strip of seaboard, its population less than that of a single State to-day which then not even existed ; so dependent on the mother country that the word home almost meant the British isles three thousand miles across the sea, with no manufactures, with little commerce, without ships, with no military reliance except a farmer here and there, who had served a half summer in the French and Indian wars, or a damaged keg of powder and a rusty flint-lock left over from the waste of English regiments. Our fathers were then thrilling, not with the memory with which we stir so profoundly, but with the very impendence and shock of Bunker Hill and Lexington and all their portent of the bloody penalties of treason and of war threatening to slay the father and the first-born, and to devastate the little farm that thrift had earned with such hard toil. The historian and poet paint the combat and the congress, but they cannot reproduce the intensity of feeling that agitated every little village and fireside. Something of civil war, endangering our precious union as freemen, we saw in 1861, but its thunders rolled afar off, its lightning rent the murky horizon only in the distant South; and the experience it brought, appalling as it was, is not a fair test of that through which in Massachusetts our ancestors were passing a hundred years ago.

We ask you to recall the sparse settlements, the fewer streets and houses, the village inn and store, the courier on horseback, the quaint vehicles of that day, the slow transmission of news, the timidity of those who clung to the royal garment, and the enthusiasm of those who were catching the inspiration of independence. You must remember that steam had then no other mission than to sing by the kitchen fire; that electricity had but just revealed its mysterious spark on the bold knuckle of Franklin; that no piano tinkled in the parlor; that no sewing machine relieved the housewife's busy fingers; that agricultural tools and processes were rude; that hasty pudding was good fare; that the old time-piece in the corner ticked with a lazy beat as loud as the tap of a drum; that the thanksgiving turkey wasted not its fragrance in the oven of a cooking-stove, but turned on the spit over great generous fires of beech and maple; that wooden chairs, with possibly a leather bottom, were a greater luxury than sofas of plush to-day; that no loom wove cotton cloth, but men wore homespun, the product of the spinning-wheel turned by aristocratic mothers and daughters; and women were elegant in gowns that now would hardly make the puffs on the overskirt of a chambermaid. The stage-coach was a wonder; the tavern and the half-way house were alive with the cheer and bustle of arrival and departure; everybody — even the parson — drank toddy, and a flush at the end of the nose, if not an ornament, was not a reproach. The newspaper, despot of modern civilization, was in its infancy, a rare and meagre slip; and the interviewer who to-day gleans the very crumbs from your table and details your mildest domestic infelicity in the public prints, was all unconscious of his destiny as the great liar and bore of the coming century. There was no spelling book, and George Washington, who could defy a king, would have gone down before one of our primary school girls. The schoolhouse was a shed and not a palace. The plagues of Western grasshopper, lightning-rod man, and book agent, spared even to Pharaoh, still slumbered in the chrysalis of the unhappy future.

People ate from wooden bowls and pewter platters and not with silver forks. They locked their doors, if at all, with bars of wood in sockets. They slept in unwarmed rooms. In the meeting house in winter time the vapor of their breath, condensed by the frigid air, helped waft their prayers to heaven. From Saturday eve to Sunday night, a great hush and soberness were over them, and on the Sabbath they rivaled the torture of the penitent's flagellation by subjecting adult and child to the infliction of two, if not three sermons, each longer than a president's message. The great secular occasions were the training and the raising. They were a sturdy, plain, economical, and thorough people, and the night would bloom into the rosy morn were I to set forth, even if I could, half the virtues which made them the germ of so noble a growth, or half the peculiarities of fashion and of domestic arrangement, which marked their thrift, and of which the women of Hingham have procured these interesting relics.

You will see the chairs they sat in ; the tables at which they ate ; the clocks by which they rose and slept ; the caps, the shoes, the cradles, the very playthings of their petticoat childhood; the dresses they wore; their swords now eaten with rust; the spurs of Washington; the knife and fork of John Adams. You will see their miserable continental rag money — solemn warning to us to-day — inflated till the distress and riot it induced almost robbed independence of its value and made the sacrifices of the Revolution a mockery. Most perishable and yet most enduring of all, you will see the letters of business, of friendship, and affection they wrote. What volumes are in those fragile leaves, those trembling tracings of pen and ink! You will see the signatures of Washington and Knox, Lincoln, Adams, and Jefferson. As you gaze, a hundred years seem but as a day, and you stand in the very presence of the fathers of the republic amid scenes warm with their personal approach. It is the substantial and the strong which passes away; the delicate and invisible which survives. Rare are the mansions of brick and wood our fathers raised; but their words still live and burn. Their material surroundings have almost utterly perished, so that only a relic here and there, left in some attic or preserved by some kindly antiquarian, remains to win the imagination backward; but their spirit, their thought, their intellectual and moral achievements, have crystallized into the great foundation stones on which the structure of to-day stands with all that is best and strongest in our institutions, and are conspicuous, like the pedestal of a monument, in the eternal truths of the declaration of independence, in the constitutions of the commonwealth and the nation, in the very votes that slumber in the fading records of the clerks of this and of many another Massachusetts town. These are living nerves that never die, that to-day are as vital as in 1775; that in 1775 were as vital as to-day.

This suggests the real purpose of this centennial tea party. It is not alone an occasion for merry-making, though it includes that; it is not a mere tribute to departed days and heroes; it is a recognition of living issues and principles which were indeed illustrated in the grand events and noble souls of the American revolution, but which demand now as then, which a hundred years hence will demand as now, our allegiance and service.

I am not of those who magnify the past at the expense of the present. I believe we have not fallen below the standard of our forefathers, but on the contrary have added to their growth. Civilization is not only a hundred years older, but a hundred years better and grander than it was in their day. The thinker, the scientist, the scholar, the divine has stridden worlds beyond their horizon; our schools are of a scope and generosity such as they never dreamed of. John Harvard builded his college better than he knew; our education, wide as the world in its sources and diffusion, stretches broad across, above, and below the narrow gamut of their instruction; science and social progress, the arts, literature, the amenities of life, have all expanded in America out of the limits of the former century into freer range; even our politics, taking into view the tremendous growth of political prizes, demands, interests, and responsibilities, are as pure as theirs; and if there are fewer examples of individual greatness, — though I doubt this, with such names as leap at once to the mind in the church, the bar, the congress, the executive chair, in business, in every walk of life at the present time, — certainly our general level is superior. With familiarity comes contempt, and it is easy and vulgar eloquence that vilifies the present and immediate. Assuredly we have no example of treason so base as that of Benedict Arnold, or of a spirit meaner than that which, in the Continental Congress and army, barked at the heels of the Continental commander-in-chief; or of a corrupter state of affairs than Jefferson deplored. Uncompromising Sam Adams is matched in Phillips, Garrison, or Sumner; nor can the past exhibit a purer martyr than Abraham Lincoln or a nobler hero than John A. Andrew.

All this, too, though all this time our population has been multiplying, our life growing more artificial, our forms more intricate and liable to abuse, and our ports opening as an asylum to the inflow of foreign populations. If we seem to see more crime and corruption, it is because the area is larger, and the sharp criticism which holds the citizen and the official to their duty is keener and more searching. In the matter of temperance we are more abstinent and alive to its necessity; in health we are better educated; in the one item of human slavery it is boast enough for this generation that it has eradicated a cancer which the last century fostered and permitted.

Yet true it is that the moral level is still a thousand times too low. All this material and intellectual progress has brought with it only a greater responsibility; and no American, who rises to the true appreciation of his citizenship, and of his descent from the heroes of 1775, can for a moment reflect upon the startling and portentous expansion of the nation, its vast wants, its intricate and ponderous machinery of government, its temptations to corruption in business, in politics, in every relation, without feeling that the great need, the one thing to enforce everywhere, is the personal accountability of every citizen for the welfare and dignity and high character of his country, and for taking care, in the noble language of the Roman fathers, that the republic suffer no detriment. We cannot too earnestly impress this duty or concentrate too many influences in its behalf. For this reason it is indeed well to keep always before our eyes what is sterling, what is best in the past. Happy is it in the providence of God that the dead past does bury its dead, but — though the poet forgot to add it — keeps alive its living; that it buries the dead lies, the dead meanness, cowardice, treason, the dead infidelity, sin, and folly, the dead men that have sunk into benign oblivion; but that whatever was heroic and divine, whatever was pure gold, whatever true man lived, whatever good and patriotic deed was done or word spoken, wherever a Washington gathered into his form all the beauty of manliness, into his soul all the grandeur of an exalted life, all these the past preserves forever fresh and immortal. I doubt not that Jesus — the divine poet — meant this when he bade the disciple let the dead bury their dead. Well may time drop the curtain hastily over its own decay. It is the spirit we want, not the form; the germ and not the husk; the principle and not the event; the thought and not the man. It were nonsense to pay tribute to the memory of the Revolution, or to celebrate this Centennial year for its own sake or for any other purpose than to utilize the past in the future, to project the lessons, the experience, the better soul of the past into the soul of the future, to make it also better and grander. In the light of mere narrative and boast, the battle, the victory, the congress are idle tales that are told; they might as well have been the fictions of the Æneid, or the pictures of the novelist; and but for the aid which our dull imaginations get from material associations and the touch of flesh and blood, the personages of Shakespeare are more real than the signers of the Declaration of Independence; the Ivanhoe of romance is a knight better known to us than the youthful Lafayette crossing the ocean to couch his lance in the cause of freedom; and Colonel Thomas Newcome and Mr. Pickwick have exerted a more personal influence in forming the character of the Christian gentleman than Dr. Johnson or Washington Irving. But as examples of what true men have achieved and of what we may therefore achieve as well, — as exhibiting virtue, not as the mere ideal of the poet, but as the substantial consummation of a noble life actually lived, the characters and deeds of our ancestors are very fountains of inspiration. Therefore let us dwell on the delightful picture that history and poetry and the refining touch of a century, obscuring all ignobler elements, have drawn so vividly for us of their patriotism, their courage, their wisdom, their purpose, and achievement. Let us note how, in those days, the religious element entered into all the relations of life and of public affairs. Not the mere form of prayer and sermon, the sanctimonious habit and look; but that religious element which we feel in the character of Washington, which recognizes the dependence of the human soul — not as a speculation or a philosophy, but as an actual, experimental, daily necessity — upon an overruling Providence, acting always under a sense of its awful supervision, looking to it for a better inspiration and a loftier purpose. I feel profoundly that this is an element in the past which we cannot afford to lose; that as a nation, as communities, as individuals, it is vital that this faith, this dependence, this one great link, binding the weak to the infinite, lifting the soul above meaner levels to its duty to God, be recognized as the very needle of the social and political compass. Let us note, too, especially in these days, when the words union and reconciliation are the very dove and olive-leaf after the deluge of civil war, the generous co-operation and whole-heartedness that led the colonies, in spite of great distances, of remote interests, of diverse faiths and descent, to unite as one man in a holy cause; nay, that united the whole world in a step forward. We may view the American Revolution in a double aspect, — as the consolidation of thirteen colonies into a single empire, as also one of the progressive lifts of the civilization of the world at large.

In either view, then, recall those eventful days a hundred years ago this summer evening. All British America is aroused and uniting. Within the lines that circle from Dorchester to Chelsea are the bivouacs and camp-fires of the patriots, of the Puritan, and the cavalier, — of the sons of the Huguenots, the Highlanders, the Dutch burghers, — of the children of Erin and of Africa. The soldiers who fought at Bunker Hill — their laurels already won — represent all the four provinces that constitute New England. In command are Stark and Sullivan from New Hampshire, Knowlton and Putnam from Connecticut, and from Rhode Island, Greene, the noblest soldier of the war, dying in poverty soon after its close, and lying to-day in an unknown grave. The story of Prescott's stern resistance runs like wildfire. At Cambridge, on the 3d of July, under the great elm that bears his name and could almost hide his whole army under its shade, Washington takes command of the continental forces. To his call for supplies flow generous responses from New York, Pennsylvania, New Jersey, South Carolina, and remotest Georgia. In August — this very month — come into camp fourteen hundred riflemen from Virginia, under command of Daniel Morgan, a magnificent creation of bone and sinew, experienced in the Indian wars, and destined to a glorious career in the army. Maryland, her soldiers always veterans in the years that follow, gathers recruits beyond the Alleghanies and sends them merrily over the mountains to be in at the siege of Boston. A regiment from Pennsylvania follows. These brave cousins from sister provinces come marching hundreds of miles in hunting shirts and moccasins, unerring in the use of the rifle, and uniting the soldier and the woodsman. In no quarter glows a more generous enthusiasm than in the Carolinas, where, fired by the example of Lexington, patriots rise in support of the patriot's cause, and where, romance blending with history, Flora McDonald, heroine of Scott's first novel, who in her youth had risked her life to save that of her prince, Charles Edward, after the battle of Culloden, now in her womanly maturity, a pioneer with her Highland husband in North Carolina, is especially active in her patriotic efforts, and yet is only one of a thousand daring souls. Indeed, since the sun went down on the night of the 17th of June, the struggle has ceased to be a local one. It is no longer a matter of Boston Common or the stores at Concord. It has become a nation's cause, and the whole land, small in numbers, but vast in extent, springs with a united front and purpose to the defense of freedom, to the resistance of tyranny, to the impending, though yet unacknowledged assertion of national independence. By this twelfth day of August, not the Massachusetts minute men, but a continental army, beleaguers Boston, commanded by a son of Virginia, its ranks recruited from nearly every colony; its heart inspired with encouragement, and its achievements watched with eager interest from Georgia to the St. Lawrence; and the ardor of its captains fully supplemented by the earnest spirits who, at their various homes, by pen

and voice, are spreading the flame of liberty, as Clan Al-
pine speeds the torch at the rising of the clan, and are
cultivating among the colonists that common enthusiasm
which shall afterwards develop into a more perfect union.
At Philadelphia sits the immortal Congress, in which
Adams, Jefferson, Franklin, Rutledge, and representatives from every province inspire in one another the
mounting resolution, which, to their eternal fame, though
at the risk of the hangman's rope, lifts them, a year later,
up to the Declaration of Independence.

This is all trite, but it is worth while to remember that
the American Revolution was the birth of our Federal
Union; that that Union, long before it was expressed in
constitutional form, existed in the spontaneous and generous sympathy which sustained the Continental Congress
itself; which bore the brunt of the war; which year after
year sent soldiers into the weary and disheartening cam-
paigns and raised supplies to keep them; and which endured poverty and death and fire and sword that the cause
of American freedom might prevail. Without that union
in sympathy first and in political coherence afterwards,
our independence could not have been achieved. And
now, after the gloomy hurricane of civil war that has just
passed over us, shall we not do, what to-day we can, to
renew the same responsive sympathy that wrought so
much a hundred years ago? Our civil war was simply the
common cost we all paid for suffering a false principle, an
unsound element, to inhere in our political union. It is a
striking example of the utter inexpediency of mere expediency, of the penalties that are sure to follow any com-
promise that recognizes and perpetuates a wrong. That
common cost we have paid in blood, in treasure, in the
best lives of the nation; and the next step is the new re-

union on the loftier plane instead of the old union on the lower one. How the imagination expands as it anticipates the results of this reunion, as it foresees the great, magnificent South with its fertile fields, its immense seaboard, its noble rivers, its rich mountains and valleys, its fruitful climate, opening to the development of free labor, expanding under systems of free schools, its fetters forged by its own hands broken by ours, its sons reuniting with its ancient friends at the North in the glorious achievement of the highest civilization and prosperity, as a hundred years ago in the achievement of victory on battlefields in behalf of political independence. Blessed be these centennial days that have brought to the monument at Bunker Hill the troops of a Southern State, laying garlands of flowers at its base and planting the palmetto of Carolina by the Northern pine; and that have seen the soldiers of the rebellion taught in the streets of Boston, what neither the newspaper, nor Congress and the National Executive, nor five years of bloody revolution could teach them, — what nothing but their own eyes could convince them of, — the fact that Massachusetts, as generous as she is powerful, has had no other purpose than to do justly and to love mercy; that she has never felt the spirit of vindictiveness, but stands always ready to renew the attachment of the fathers; but that never was an attempt so wicked, so full of folly and delusion, as rebellion against that government which the men of 1775, North and South, sacrificed so much to found and perpetuate. This year seals the grander and second consolidation of America. And narrow is the soul and mischievous the memory that would recall the bitterness of civil strife, save as a warning against the errors that begot it, or that would utter one word or do one act to stay the blessed work of reconciliation.

But even this is not the whole significance of the American Revolution; this is not all we commemorate in these centennial occasions. The American Revolution was a step in the progress of the whole world, an impulse for which we should not be grateful to our American ancestors North and South alone. Englishmen ourselves, not the least of our debt do we owe to England herself, whose tendencies for a thousand years had been reaching toward political enfranchisement; whose finer statesmen, poets, scholars, and divines had always fostered the spirit that in 1775 found also expression in the dauntless faith and bold purpose of Sam and John Adams; whose better minds even in the height of the war were with us; whose orators, like Chatham, Burke, Camden, and many others, espoused our cause and within the very walls of the British parliament uttered eloquent and fearless appeals in our behalf; whose generals, like Howe and Carleton, even when leading her armies against us, could not be indifferent to the common ties that had linked us together so long; and whose soldiers, though arrayed against their own countrymen, yet by prolonging the war till the cement of union and independence grew hard, became unconscious agencies in the accomplishment of a revolution, that indeed lost England her colonies, but gained for her and for the world a successful example of republican institutions, of a popular rebellion against injustice vindicated, and of the humblest citizen made in his political and social rights the peer of monarch and magnate. The intelligence of England to-day regards our Revolution not as a victory over her, which as a mere victory of arms and military force we could scarce have secured, but as an achievement in civil liberty and growth the merit and fruit of which she shares with us, as the mother

glories and shares in the attainments of her child. No
more loving or appreciative picture of Washington has
been drawn than that by Thackeray in "The Virginians."

Among the relics here to-night is the red coat of a
British soldier found at Bunker Hill. For aught I know
some burly Yorkshireman threw it off that hot June afternoon and, frightened by a Yankee blunderbuss aimed at
the white of his eye, ran away to become another day the
ancestor of that great-hearted preacher [Robert Collyer]
whose home and warmest welcome are in the land his
grandsire fought; who knows not whether he is of England or America, because he is of both; and who perhaps will tell you to-night, in his own inimitable and
cordial way, that so welded are the two nations in all
good and generous things, that loyalty to either is loyalty
to each. Nor must we forget the enthusiasm our struggle awoke all through Europe, — the aid that came from
foreign powers, whether in the undisguised sympathy of
Russia and Frederick the Great, or in the substantial
contribution of armies, ships, money, and munitions of
war that poured from the lavish hand of France and less
from Spain and Holland. And last, we must not forget
those individuals who, fired by the story of our wrongs,
emulating the examples of chivalry and romance, sped to
our rescue: Lafayette, a boy of seventeen, forsaking his
tender wife, abandoning his high position in the royal
army and court, giving from his princely fortune to clothe
and feed our soldiers, the bosom friend of Washington,
the adopted child of America; De Kalb accompanying
him to lay down his life for us at the battle of Camden;
Steuben who taught our soldiers discipline; Kosciusko
the Polish patriot; Pulaski, killed at the siege of Savan-
nah; and a host of others, no doubt animated by love of

adventure and hope of fame, but underneath all recognizing the grandeur of the cause to which they offered their lives. With all these elements in and out of America involved, it was indeed one of those epochs in the world's history when the onward flow of progress at a particular time and in a particular place rose into a tidal wave. In this broad view there is no occasion that is entirely our own and not the world's. It would be a narrow thing to celebrate the Centennial of the birth of American Independence if we did not recognize its results outside of America. God works in no limited way. All nature responds to the remotest touch. Not a wave of your hand but the poles vibrate and the moons of Jupiter yield a graceful response. Not a child cries in its sleep at nightfall but some bird at the antipodal sunrise, ignorant whence the wave that tinkles in its ear, awakes and sings its morning song. And so in these grander events, none of them occurs but the world's history, its progress for good or bad, is affected. It is the world's centennial, and that I am soaring into no extravagance, see how a practical people propose to celebrate it.

It is proposed to celebrate it by a World's Exhibition and Gathering in Philadelphia in the year 1876. To aid this great enterprise is the object of this tea party to-night, and of a hundred others that will occur in the various towns of this Commonwealth. Certainly in no town more fittingly than in Hingham, the home of General Lincoln, — now most illustrious of American names, — on whose shoulder rested the hand of Washington; whose foresight had so much to do with the triumph at Saratoga, though his wounds deprived him of participation in it; who received the sword of Cornwallis at Yorktown; whose aides, Shute, not yet through college, Rice, Baylies, Barker, were of the blood of your best families; and who quelled Shay's Rebellion less by military skill than by his prudent sense; the town where Lafayette, at once boy and statesman, major-general and knight-errant, supped on bread and milk and patted the head of a little child, who lived to become the mother of our distinguished village historian; the town, whose honored meeting-house, the most ancient in the land, already old when the Adamses were children, is about to celebrate its second centennial, linking its worshipers of to-day with those who worshiped in its walls a hundred years before our independence; the town where — not its least distinction — lived John A. Andrew, who may well rank with any patriot of Revolutionary fame. It is an occasion perfected by the women of the Revolutionary sort, patriotic as Abigail Adams or Flora McDonald, without whose help nothing in modern times proceeds, whether it be war or picnics, education or a tea party, — nothing except it be the ballot box, from which I am afraid we exclude them not because we doubt but because we are sure of their ample ability to take it into their own hands. It is an occasion preliminary to the greater occasion at Philadelphia another year, but its object is the same, to awaken the memories of the past, to promote the admiration of patriotic virtues, the love of fatherland, the value of union among ourselves, the unity of Massachusetts, of the United States, of America, with the world. In the Centennial at Philadelphia the scenes of a hundred years ago will be repeated. Again the leading spirits of North and South and East and West will come together over the mountains and rivers with all their variety of dress and habit and production. Again will cross the sea the British forces emulous for the contest, invading the ports of

Boston and New York, marching over the field of Brandy-
wine, through the historic Jerseys and down from Canada
by the lakes and the Hudson to capture us at Philadelphia. Again will pour in upon us the resources of France
and Germany and the enthusiastic interest of all Europe.
But there will be no bloodshed; the sword has been
beaten into a plowshare and the spear into a pruning-
hook. Instead of the scream of the deadly shell is the
whistle of the locomotive, emblem of the magnificent proportions of the trade, transportation, and commerce of
the nineteenth century! Instead of the roar of musketry
are the din of looms and the buzz of machinery singing
songs of the home, the fireside, the happy circles of domestic cheer! Instead of the bugle blast to sound the
charge is the music of the orchestra to lead the dance
and of the civic festival to inspire the orator! Instead
of the groans of wounded and dying foemen are the
friendly voices of a million hearts united in a common
enjoyment and zest of the glad jubilee of all the nations. The contests and the laurels will be those of peace
and not of war, whose bloody victories we glorify not
for themselves, but because their justification is in their
blessed fruition of peace. Is not the century worth something, which terminates like this, whose hundredth year
blossoms with reconciliation, reunion, material prosperity,
and the cordial coöperation of the peoples of the earth
in celebrating the triumphs of peaceful arts, of useful
manufactures, of beneficent industries, and a high civilization? Let us see that patriots are at the head of our
forces, that our Massachusetts maintains her old continental preëminence in the field and the council, and that
Hingham's quota fails not for the first time. Let the Centennial at Philadelphia give to the world an impulse in

the grand progress of the age worthy of that it there received on the Fourth of July, 1776, when Washington was our standard bearer; when Franklin was the wisest man after Diogenes; and since when, all the leaders of the infant republic, its warriors in the field, its statesmen in the congress, have seemed to us, looking at them through the glorifying mist of the century, so grand and heroic that with fond exaggeration we say, there were giants in the earth in those days.

ADDRESS

AT THE DEDICATION OF THE WALLACE AND CONVERSE MEMORIAL
LIBRARY BUILDINGS, AT FITCHBURG AND MALDEN, JULY 1 AND
OCTOBER 1, 1885.

THIS is one of those occasions which illustrate the
poverty and inexpressiveness of words and things, and
the inexhaustible riches of the ideal. We cheat ourselves
with the delusion that to-day we dedicate the magnificent
walls and graceful proportions of a public library building wrought out of wood and stone. Not so. Its appointments are but symbols, noble and exquisite in themselves but faint and fleeting in comparison with that
deeper reality, — that reality of ideality, inexpressible in
human language or architectural material, — the reality
of the love of the human heart, of the charity of human
brotherhood, of the eternal progress of the human mind,
of the mastery of human industry, — of all which they
are only the suggestion. If you would therefore trace
the true sources of this splendid edifice, you will go, not
to any plan of architect, but into the sacred recesses of
the human heart. If you would seek its purpose, you will
find it in no monumental impression upon the public eye,
or against the background of the blue heaven, but in the
generous, unrestricted treasures of instruction and soulful
delight, which from this time henceforth it will pour out
upon this community. If you would learn its lesson, it is
that of the march of a civilization of all the people which
stops short at no milestone of progress, and in which it is

itself only a step. If you would follow its construction, you will think not alone of the generosity that gave or the brain that planned it, but of the varied and busy hands, representing every branch of mechanical art and honest labor, which have contributed to its rise from the first blow of the pickaxe to the nicest touch of the carver's artistic chisel. You, with a citizen's pride, have often gazed at its impressive architecture and read the poem of its beautiful interior finish. I, with a stranger's curiosity and pleasure, have visited it. I looked upon its massive walls, — its heavy blocks of brown sandstone, — its carved ornamentation. I entered its doors and stood alone under its arches. I saw the interminable series of vacant shelves, soon to bend beneath their precious weight of literature, — the panelings of quartered oak, — the great generous fireplace, suggestive of the old-time New England hospitality, — the tables yet bare, — the art gallery waiting for its decoration of sculpture and painting. Yet not alone. For, looking back through the vista of the past year, I saw those spaces alive with the workmanship of American industry, ringing with the sound of the hammer, the trowel, and the saw, and I realized the noblest feature of our American system in this, — that the very labor and toil, even the crudest and humblest, which wrought and built and went into this library building, are themselves the beneficiaries which are to profit by it, and henceforth to enjoy its inestimable blessings, — building, indeed, better than they knew. Happy and fortunate the benefactors, who, touching in the chamber of their hearts an electric knob, thus set in motion the industrial activities which bear such fruit, such mercy a thousand times blessed, for giver and recipient alike ; but I do them only justice, I am sure, and express only their thought, when I say that their happiest satisfaction is that this gift of theirs represents not their contribution alone, but the contribution also of many of those in whose behalf they erect and dedicate it.

But looking forward through the vista of the years to come, I was conscious still more of another realization. The mellow afternoon sun threw its glory on carved columns and groaning shelves. The evening lights flashed down their splendor. The alcoves swarmed. The tables were laden. The walls were hung with works of art. The sculptured marble seemed instinct with the breath of life. Best of all, the aisles and niches were alive with humanity. Men and women, little children, school-boys and girls, rich and poor, the man of leisure and the workman coming from his toil, came in and out and drank freely of the waters of life. For the value of this edifice is not in its architectural proportions and its cunning workmanship of frame and finish. It is in the magnificent use, the generous and ennobling service to which it is consecrated. Literally a treasure-house of knowledge, an inexhaustible mine of education, — the monopoly of no man or body of men, — it is thrown wide open for generations to come to the free common resort and possession of the people. A Roman emperor, wasting the substance of the state in selfish wars, or to feed his own luxurious depravity, tickled his starving subjects with now and then the pageant of a procession, the blood of the gladiatorial arena, or the distribution of corn as modern travelers throw coins to Italian beggars. To-day an American citizen, one in the front ranks of a free and equal community, architect of his own deserved and liberal fortune, loyal to the needs and ambition of his common citizenship, paying tribute to those foundations of the

American polity which are the general intelligence and virtue of the people, wresting nothing from others, but giving of his own, opens in the heart of your city an unfailing well-spring of public education and delight. He smites the hard rock of this intense American industrial and material system, and lo! the waters of life, rich with nutrition for the whole intellectual and moral nature, gush forth. They crystallize in a public library and art-building that shall insure the range of published study and inquiry, free reading-rooms, and the treasures of science, art, and literature. If you would measure its value you will not reckon the land, or stone, or wood, or even the more than hundred thousand dollars that have gone into its construction. You would measure it, as I am sure the givers do, by looking along the expanding vista of the time to come. You will here see some future Bunyan, of rapt imagination, saved by its illumination of inquiry and truth from those terrors and hideous fancies of religious frenzy which, until the serenity of a loftier faith came to him, drove the young tinker of Bedford almost to the madness of despair, though I fear you would lose the vivid allegory of "The Pilgrim's Progress." You will picture here the eager face of some later Abraham Lincoln, burnt brown with the sunshine of the farm, some Henry Wilson hastening from the shoemaker's lap-stone, some mechanic from his bench, the men and women of your industries, — all here enjoying a society of refinement and culture, a communion with the master-spirits of all time, an education in all the humanities. The myths of classic time will here be the homeliest of facts. The goddess of all knowledge will spring, full equipped, from the cleft of a mightier than pagan godhead, — the open volume of a book. The winged Pegasus that bears its rider to the stars will be the leaves, — more precious than the sibyl's, — the leaves on these clustering shelves, from which no idle wind will flutter them. The sweetest poetry of written verse will be but as homely prose to the poetry of the actuality of this scene. Maud Muller's "wish that she hardly dared to own, for something better than she had known," will be realized in a companionship and surrounding such as the Judge's hand, had he conferred it, never could have brought. The "barefoot boy" will indeed have more than the "million-dollared" can buy. In the town in which I live we have, like you, a public library, founded by the munificence of a citizen. Walking from it one perfect September day, I overtook a child slow sauntering before me. In her dress was the evidence of that pathetic poverty which seeks to hide its destitution with the mother's midnight needle and the prudent patch. Her broken and over-crushed shoes, a mile too large, were the evident gratuity of charity. But under each arm was a library book, and in her hands a third, held wide open, which she read as she walked. Passing, I caught, under the torn hat-brim, that intelligent child-face, traced with a pensive sadness, which is so often seen among the children of the poor. Apparently my salutation woke the blue eyes, which trembled up, from a dream in which all consciousness of the actual time and place had been lost, and in which the soul was living in the transcendent ranges of an upper world, — the world of the aspiring imagination, — the world of literature and mind, — the world in which all the good and wise and lovely are our society. Is it nothing to have conferred such a blessing on one of God's little ones, — to have made such an one the messenger of glad tidings to some humble household, which, under the gifts she was bringing,

would gladden into happiness and instruction? Measure
the value of your public library! Suppose for one moment that its contents were blotted out; that the world of
books were consumed; that the records of history, science,
and fiction — the vehicles of fact and event, of discovery
and truth, of imagination and poetry — were a lost art.
Why, we live less in the present than in the past; less in
ourselves than in the atmosphere and society which history
and literature have created! What man in this region of
the earth is so open to you in his heart and thought and
dreams as David, or Emerson, or Thackeray? Of what
man here do you know so much as of Washington or
Bonaparte? In whose poetic tendernesses or aspirations
do you find half the sympathy you find in Longfellow
and Whittier? What drama of domestic or public life is
half so familiar as that of Walter Scott and Shakespeare?
Which of your neighbors can hold you with the illuminated talk-torrent of Macaulay? Is there nothing, too, to
be said in praise of an agency which thus sweeps our vision
and our interests out of the small and inbreeding confines
of local friction and gossip into these world-wide and
time-wide ranges of creative power? Here in his single
hand the citizen grasps the universe. Here he listens
to the debates of Congress. Here he watches the move-
ments of armies on Afghan or Egyptian fields. Here he
studies the diplomatic contests of Europe, and looks over
their shoulders into the hands of negotiating ambassadors.
Here he is member of the senates of the world. Here
he traces the comet in the sky, or cuts Isthmian canals, or
explores the icy terrors of the pole, or in the exquisite
realm of the imagination sings with the poet and inquires
with the philosopher. Here solitude becomes society.
The soul is supreme master of the realm, and man recog-

nizes that he is a god. It is more than a school, — more than education; it is absolute possession. The scholar is king, and every citizen is a scholar. His soul inherits the earth. No devil tempts him, yet his are all the kingdoms of the world, and all the glory of them.

While this building is unique in its purpose it is yet — to the honor of our American civilization be it said — only in the line and easy evolution of our New England system. It is as much a flower of the Pilgrim and Puritan seed, as much a part of the providential scheme of the Mayflower and of John Winthrop's landing, as much fused with the flavor of Harry Vane, as much a result of that vote of 1647, which declared that "learning should not be buried in the graves of our forefathers," as is Harvard College, or our common school system, or as if every stone under its roof, every book on its shelves, every picture upon its walls, had been in the mind's eye of the founders of Massachusetts. Still more does it partake of the elements of our later consummations, — our marvelous industrial growths. In its very amplitude it yet embodies the idea of that homely saving economy, that intelligent thrift, that careful provision for future needs, which characterize New England. It embodies the idea of those great agencies and massings of skilled and citizenized labor, which at once employ a multitude of hands and at the same time stimulate as many activities of invention and brain, and so combine manual toil and intellectual genius in that splendid union of which our national institutions are at once the cause and the result. Thence comes the steady expansion of general prosperity; the increasing thriving of the body of the people; the greater independence and comfortable self-support of families; their homes in separate dwellings of their own, into each of which flows a growing tide of refinement, culture, and amusement; the enlargement of public education, and the advancing standard of the schools; the saturation of the press, and the consequent connection of local life with cosmopolitan interests; along with these the accumulation by individuals here and there of large fortunes to a good purpose, provided they be not wrenched out of others' earnings, but, on the contrary, constitute, in the very process of their accumulation, the fund of others' earnings; and then at last the public spirit in some such individual, which, hardly more by his own impulse than by the commanding general sentiment of which he is almost the involuntary servant and expression, appropriates a part of his fortune back to the public use and service. Can there be a finer tribute to labor than that thus, by its own inherent law of action, operating under our institutions of political freedom, it ministers to its own nobler needs even in the very act of its own exercise, whether executing the designs of the nicest skill and most scientific mechanisms, or faithfully hewing wood and drawing water, — its own hand providing for the education of its head and the refinement of its heart? Behold a marvel more wondrous than any tale of magical conjuration or oriental myth! For not in the closet of the student, not in the shade of the cloister, not in the vista of the poet, not on the campus of a college; but straight out of the busiest, most intense, hardest-headed and hardest-handed material concentration of industrial, manufacturing, money-making, labor-employing forces and enterprise, springs this fair flower of the gentlest humanities, this grace of art, this fountain of letters, this frozen song of architecture! What is this but poetry and religion, — the tribute of the creature to God, — the obeisance of matter to mind,

of toil to rest, of the hard, practical forces to their master, the spirit of thought and vision, — the recognition of
that spiritual, that mental and moral sovereignty which
is the divine equality of all the children of God and to
which all lower life with its inequalities of circumstance,
its dross of riches, and its grime of toil, is the shell of the
chambered nautilus !

Yes, this building typifies the true communism.   Here
is the most precious wealth, the best treasures, — as far
above all material mint and anise and cummin as the
clouds above the earth, — and all is for all alike.   Ah !
that is the sweet assurance which letters, books, art, literature, and the whole range of intellectual life give to the
world.   The vicissitudes of fortune, the fluctuations of
business, the rise and fall of stocks and prices, the suc-
cessions of good times and hard times, the inequalities of
material lot which are inevitable, nay, are the very soil
and stimulus of individual and social bettering,— all these
cannot invade this realm, and he who invests his happiness in this security will never suffer bankruptcy.   The
refinement and riches of study and letters, open alike to
all, is one of the best lessons of this dedication, summon-
ing the whole world to its communism of goods.   The
wealth of Crœsus could not gather out of the past, out of
the resources of intellectual treasure, what this new inclosure will hold.   And yet all which this inclosure will
hold will be, not the monopoly of Crœsus, not his exclusive of you and me, but our common possession ; and the
poorest child will here come and here command to his side
statesmen, poets, orators, warriors, all the greatness of
human career, to minister to his pleasure, companionship,
and instruction.   Under that vault will echo no song of
the shirt, but the poet's song of the woods, of enriched

solitude, of the mind's paradise. And here, whatever his garb or trade or circumstance, the citizen student will learn that there is nothing so great as his own soul; and that the master-spirits of all time, who have inspired all the volumes of all the libraries, exist not so much in themselves as in their own ideals and in the ideals of those who have, with varying exaggeration and mirage, interpreted their deeds or words, reproducing for us poet, prophet, leader, and inspirer, not out of those limits and facts of certain years of our Lord, which are shifting guess-work, but out of those subtle and worshipful conceptions and mountings of the human mind, which are the eternal and only truth. He will learn that to him these great spirits are of most interest as even thus they reflect his own highest ideals and help him realize them. Nothing to him the royal robes or fragrant palaces of Solomon, but everything to him David's agony of pain or tumult of aspiration, because they are the pain and aspiration of his own heart.

In the engrossments of every-day life, few of us appreciate what a *universal* blessing a library is. I have been surprised and delighted in my observation of our towns, to find how generally people of all conditions of life and degrees of means depend upon the public library, — of how many a sick room it is the light, — of how many a poor man's home it is the cheer, — of how much leisure and ennui it is the relief, — and how thoroughly well-informed and well-read the community is made by its resources. Little does he know of our New England culture who thinks it confined to the select, or who from a thorough acquaintance with New England homes has not almost invariably found in them a wealth and variety of book-study, an acquaintance with the field of authors and their works, a literary gleaning and harvest, which a characteristic reticence often hides, but which are as surely there as the waters, whose flow is in winter time unheard, are under their mantle of ice and snow. But this fact of the eager and general use of the public library only the more emphatically suggests that while such a resource is a mighty instrument for delight and for good, we should not forget that it may be made an instrument, also, for evil. It is no small responsibility that will fall on those, who shall have this trust in their keeping, to select the fare it is to minister from its shelves, lest it demoralize rather than improve the public tone. We are nowadays especially careful what is the quality of the water we supply or the food we distribute from the great resources of our metropolitan centres. Let us be as careful of the intellectual and moral supply which determines—and which, under the incalculable influence of a public library, so much determines — the literary material of the people, — the procedures, not into their mouths, but out of them, — the issues of the heart.

I congratulate you upon the completion and dedication of this splendid building. It will be an unfailing spring of public instruction. It will teach the harmony and mutual dependence of our common interests. It will be a lesson of true citizenship. It is the tribute of industrial activities to the genius of letters and art and to the sovereignty of the soul. It is an inspiration to labor and to the spirit of progress. To you and to your children it will be an endeared memorial of those who gave it. In no shaded seclusion, but here, — here in the heart of your city and of its all-enriching industries, — stands their monument, alike characteristic of their generosity and of its steadily expanding public spirit and demand.

GOVERNOR ANDREW.

WRITTEN FOR " HINGHAM IN THE CIVIL WAR, 1876," AND READ AT THE DINNER OF THE COMMERCIAL CLUB, PARKER HOUSE, BOSTON, JANUARY 19, 1895.

HINGHAM has the proud distinction of having been the home of John Albion Andrew, governor of Massachusetts during the entire period of the rebellion, and of now, in accordance with the wish he once expressed before the citizens of Hingham, tenderly cherishing in her soil his sacred ashes. It is fitting that his name should stand at the head of the list of her heroic dead.

It is unnecessary to give more than the barest biographical outline of one whose life and services are already a part of the national literature, imprinted on its brightest pages. He was born of worthy New England stock, at South Windham, in the State of Maine, May 31, 1818. The comfortable circumstances of his father procured him a good academical education and a collegiate course at Brunswick. He was a glad, wholesome, noble boy, with open face and curly head, and a brave, generous, and buoyant heart, fond of history, reading widely, with a taste for poetry and elegant literature, with no exalted rank as a plodding scholar, but with always a tendency towards broad views and humane sentiments. Even in those days, the anti-slavery cause had touched his heart; and the faint whisper of the approaching storm was awakening his pulses to that love of freedom and respect for human rights which so signally found expression in his later life.

In 1837 Andrew entered the law office of Henry H. Fuller, Esq., of Boston. He pursued for twenty years the ordinary course of his profession, making now and then a stump speech or a literary oration, and constantly rising in practice and reputation. In December, 1848, he married Eliza Jones Hersey of this town, whom he had met at an anti-slavery fair in Boston; and from that period, for a great part of the time, he resided in Hingham. Here was his home, here children were born unto him, here he walked to church and sang the familiar hymns and taught the Sunday school. Here his rare and sweet social qualities surrounded him with friends who loved and admired him; and here his generous nature, his fondness for natural scenery, his love of children, and his strong social attachments, brought him some of the happiest hours of his life.

While residing in Hingham, Andrew was nominated for State senator, but defeated. He had as yet had no entrance into political service. Nevertheless, he was daily becoming better known as an intelligent advocate of progress, and for his strong anti-slavery sentiments. In 1854 he bravely defended the parties arrested for the rescue of Anthony Burns, and in 1857 was chosen to the General Court as representative of the Sixth Ward of Boston. In this arena he rose at once to distinction. Brought into conflict with Caleb Cushing, one of the astutest and most powerful debaters and thinkers of the whole country, he carried off the victory in the bitter struggle over the removal of Judge Loring. In 1859 he unflinchingly presided at the stormy meeting in Tremont Temple, for the relief of John Brown's suffering family, declaring that, whether Brown's enterprise at Harper's Ferry were right or wrong, " John Brown himself is right." In 1860 he was a delegate to the Chicago presidential convention, and contributed to the nomination of Abraham Lincoln; and in 1861, having been elected, by a sort of spontaneous impulse of the heart of the Commonwealth, as the one fit man for its magistracy, took his seat as governor of the State. In April, the rebellion already at its outburst, came the call for arms; and, as if Providence had raised him up for the place, Andrew responded to it with that electric promptness, that magnetic fervor, that soulful devotion, which, from that day forward till the end of the war, animated him under all circumstances, and imparted to the people at large the enthusiasm of his own ardent nature. His great heart breathed in that now historic telegram to the Mayor of Baltimore: " I pray you to let the bodies of our Massachusetts soldiers, dead in Baltimore, be laid out, preserved in ice, and tenderly sent forward by express to me."

Unsuspected powers at once put forth in him, his public addresses thrilled with loftier notes, his executive energies expanded to the widest limit of his countless duties and labors; the quiet citizen and plodding lawyer budded in a day into the grandest measure of the statesman and leader; and it seemed almost a dream that our good-humored neighbor was indeed the foremost governor in the Union, the most chivalrous, if not the greatest, civilian of the war. At the assembling of loyal governors at Altoona, Pa., September 24, 1862, his was the leading spirit that urged new vigor in the prosecution of the campaign. When negro regiments began to be formed, he was among the first to organize them, prescient of their efficiency and gallantry in the field. In all that could stimulate the soul of the nation, in all that could wake its patriotic fire, yet none the less in the most watchful care of the home interests of the State, of its institutions of charity and correction, he was always foremost; and the activity of his life and labors was almost superhuman. Says the Rev. Dr. Clarke, " He worked like the great engine in the heart of a steamship."

With the war, his term of office as governor expiring, he resumed the practice of the law. In 1866 he was chosen president of the New England Historic-Genealogical Society. In 1867, with the same bravery and heroism that had marked him thitherto, though against the judgment of many of his friends, he began his strenuous and able assaults upon the prohibitory law of the State. All this time his broad national reputation, his great popularity, his sound judgment, his conciliatory and liberal sentiments, were marking him as the coming man in the national councils. It seemed as if years of new usefulness lay before him. But he had finished his work.

On the 30th of October, 1867, he died at his residence in Boston. His remains were afterwards brought to Hingham; and on the 30th of October, 1869, after solemn services in the New North Church, at which he had formerly been an attendant, his Boston pastor, James Freeman Clarke, pronouncing the address, he was buried in our cemetery, near its crest, and not far from the Soldiers' Monument. At his feet are the village he loved, the branches under which he sauntered, and the picturesque stretch of the bay over which he had so many times gone to and from his home. He rests at scarce the distance of the sound of the voice from the threshold on which he stood when on the 3d of September, 1860, he addressed his fellow-citizens of Hingham, who had come to congratulate him on his nomination as governor, and in the course of his remarks spoke these hearty words : —

" I confess to you, my old neighbors, associates, and kinspeople of Hingham, that I could more fitly speak by tears than by words to-night. From the bottom of my heart for this unsought, enthusiastic, and cordial welcome I thank you. I understand — and this thought lends both sweetness and pathos to the emotions of the hour — I am here to-night among neighbors, who for the moment are all agreed to differ and all consenting to agree.

" How dear to my heart are these fields, these spreading trees, this verdant grass, this sounding shore, where now for fourteen years, through summer heat and sometimes through winter storms, I have trod your streets, rambled through your woods, sauntered by your shores, sat by your firesides, and felt the warm pressure of your hands, sometimes teaching your children in the Sunday school, sometimes speaking to my fellow citizens, always with the cordial friendship of those who differ from me oftentimes in what they thought the radicalism of my opinions. Here — here I have found most truly a home for the soul free from the cares and turmoil and responsibilities of a careful and anxious profession. Away from the busier haunts of men it has been given to me here to find a calm and sweet retreat. Here too, dear friends, I have found the home of my heart. It was into one of your families that I entered and joined myself in holy bonds of domestic love to one of the daughters of your town. Here, too, I have first known a parent's joys and a parent's sorrows. Whether you say aye or no to my selection, John A. Andrew is ever your friend."

Governor Andrew, when in Hingham, lived on the east side of Main Street, in the first house northerly from Water Street, in the Hinckley house on the same and in the Thaxter house on the opposite side of Main Street, in the old Hersey house on Summer Street, overlooking the blue water and sweet with the fragrance of clover fields, and also in the Bates house on South Street. His habits, like his nature, were simple. He loved to drive and walk; he enjoyed the breezy trips and neighborly chat of the steamer; his heart went out to children and won them; he was especially fond of conversation, full of anecdote and story, and not averse to controversial discussion. His humor and cheer were always abundant. He sang old psalms, he recited noble poems that dwelt in his memory, he was running over with the quaint history of old times and odd characters, and to the last there never faded in his breast the warm, glad enthusiasm of boyhood. His sympathies were touched as quickly as a girl's; each year he went to Maine to stand beside the grave of his mother; each day some sad woman or poor boy thanked him for his humanity, for in him the unfortunate always had a helper and friend. No heart less generous could have uttered those memorable words that expressed his great and genuine humanity: "I know not what record of sin may await me in another world; but this I do know, I never was mean enough to despise a man because he was poor, because he was ignorant, or because he was black." Add to all this his incorruptibility and honesty, his fiery patriotism, his unswerving sense of right and wrong, his pure glow in act and word, and we may trust, that, as his monument rises over his grave, it will point to the example of purposes so lofty, of a soul so magnanimous, and a mind so sound, that it will be like a beacon light to guide the way of future generations to the like achievement of the fullness of a noble life.

ORATION

Delivered before the City Council and Citizens of Boston, in the Boston Theatre, July 4, 1882.

It has seemed to you and your associates, Mr. Mayor, not unfitting, that, once in a century, a representative of the whole Commonwealth of Massachusetts should speak for this, her capital city, on Independence Day. A hundred years ago, as now, their interests, their hopes, their patriotism, were one. If Boston seemed then to stand out as the proscenium from which the curtain of the drama rose, the scene was a rapidly shifting one, and the actors came not alone, like Sam Adams and Warren and Hancock and Knox, from Boston. Like Lincoln from Hingham, Hawley from Northampton, Prescott from Pepperell, Heath from Roxbury, Gridley from Canton, John Adams from Quincy, Cobb from Taunton, Thomas from Kingston, Ward from Shrewsbury, and many others, they came from Massachusetts at large, and so identified the whole province and this its chiefest town, as they have been identified from that day to this, in the cause of liberty and progress.

Mindful, therefore, of the close relations which have thus, at all times, bound Massachusetts and Boston together, I thank you for your courtesy in inviting me to speak for you to-day, and I am here in obedience to your call. I have, as needs must be with a date celebrated now for more than a hundred anniversaries, and with its topics rehearsed till every possible variation has been exhausted, no new word to utter, no illumination to throw upon the picture. But the day is our national birthday, and even its familiar story cannot be told too often, if it shall wake each year the patriotic pulse of a people so free that they are almost unconscious of the value of their birthright of freedom, or shall educate their children to admire and emulate the high spirit, the devotion to liberty, and the love of country, which inspired the fathers and founders of the republic.

Let us, then, go back to 1776, and recall the scene and event which we now commemorate, never forgetting that they were only links in the chain which, under Providence, had been forming for centuries, and forming, let us also, in justice, remember, under English law, and under the inspiration of English hearts. The separation of the colonies from Great Britain was the result of no single cause; nor was it occasioned solely by reason of a chivalrous devotion to great principles of constitutional right or resistance to oppression. The vast territory of India, stretching over half a continent and sunk in the effeminacy and ignorance of centuries of stagnation, might for years, and may to-day, submit to the rapacious sway of the British isles, — to the terror of a superior race enriching themselves at its expense. But it was not written in the book of human destiny that the Christian civilization of the New World, the intellectual culture of New England, the growing material importance of New York and Pennsylvania, the high spirit of Virginia and the Carolinas, — nay, that any of our colonies, proud of their lineage, devoted to an independent faith, founding among themselves institutions of learning, expanding apace with the very grandeur and extent of the new continent, and year by year conscious more and more of their rapid growth and coming domain and achievement, — should hang as a dependence on an island in the Atlantic, more than that the apple, ripe and round, should cling to the stem and shrivel there in premature decay. In such a condition were the very essentials to cultivate the spirit of progress, of independent citizenship, and of the right of intelligent men, chafing under the stupid narrowness of the dolt who happened at that time to encumber the British throne, to frame their own laws, and govern themselves. The divine right of kings was not a doctrine that could thrive in such soil; and no sooner did the colonies begin, as a result of simple growth, to feel their power and to touch shoulder with one another in the sympathy of their geographical and political affinities, than independence became inevitable, and only sought occasion and apology for its own assertion.

To this end had the instruction of the mother country herself led. From her own pulpits, in the songs of her own poets, in the words of her own orators, in the progress of her own statesmanship, had for centuries been flowing influences that were lifting the individual man, leveling the accidental potentate, and proclaiming the unimportance of those who govern, and the overwhelming consequence and needs of the governed, even to the humblest citizen. It was a matter of indifference whether Burke and Chatham in England, and Adams and Otis and the town meetings of Massachusetts Bay in America, lifted their voices in a British parliament or in Faneuil Hall or Pembroke town house. The words they spoke, the sentiments they uttered, were eternal truth, and had no local habitation or name. Under these circumstances, allegiance to Great Britain was nothing but a habit and a sentiment. The moment it came face to face in conflict with a right, it went to pieces like a bubble; the moment it involved the sacrifice of a principle, the cost of injustice to the smallest penny, it was gone forever. I take it, there was nothing in British oppression that bore with special hardship on America. It is not likely that any malicious intent existed on the part of king or ministry to wrong and tyrannize over us; and both were no doubt honest in their conviction that we were a stiff-necked generation, turning in ingratitude on the parentage that had borne and nursed us. The burdens at which we actually rebelled were slight in comparison with those which we had previously borne for years, especially during the wars with France. In comparison with those which, in our recent civil war, we inflicted on ourselves, they were next to nothing. It would be hard to point to the man or community which, prior to the outbreak of bad blood, suffered greatly, in person or property, from British tyranny. Even the Declaration of Independence, which we commemorate to-day, if you carefully peruse it, lacks something of that record of specific grievances and acts of oppression, which we should expect in a statement made in justification of rebellion and treason. It would not be difficult to recite wrongs which other peoples have borne and still bear, tenfold greater than those from which we wrested independence. We who, in recent years, to suppress rebellion, willingly endured excessive governmental interference with personal rights, and who saw multitudes of new offices created, and swarms of officials and standing armies in our midst, can hardly refrain from smiling at the complaints so grandiloquently put in 1776. Nor must it be overlooked that most of these complaints were directed against the very measures which were resorted to to overcome what Great Britain regarded as treason, and which never would have been resorted to at all had our fathers been submissive. I do not mean that there were no grievances. Grievances there were, such as taxation without representation, though the actual taxes imposed were slight, and in any accustomed form the burden of them would have raised no murmur; such also as the general control and management of provincial affairs by an agency remote and indifferent. But these were grievances, not so much invented and asserted by the mother country as inherent in the very organization of her colonial system. It was the instinctive revulsion which an intelligent and not inferior people felt for the natural unfitness and injustice of the British colonial system as applied to a vigorous and self-conscious community, that made any restraint intolerable, and independence a necessity. To my mind it is infinitely more creditable to our fathers that freedom was in this way the result, not of resentment, but of a high intellectual self-respect, and of the conviction that in the maturity of their growth the time had come for them to take their own destiny into their own hands.

Once inaugurated the struggle leaped forthwith to the bitterness and desperation of the death-hug. If the provocation was lacking before, it was lacking no longer. Fatally ignorant of the pride, the English thoroughness and tenacity of her own children, Great Britain adopted measures of coercion to which they could not and would not submit. And when there came the Port Bill and the Enforcing Act and the Stamp Act, which were intended to humiliate Boston and deprive the people of their familiar privileges, and place them at the mercy of a ministerial board sitting around a table in London city, the fatal step was taken; the error could never be retrieved; estrangement was only widening with each forcible effort to heal it, and the birth of the new republic was assured. The rebellion of 1861 failed, not because of a lack of brave men and devoted effort, but because it was unfit and out of joint with the moral and physical order of the times. Unlike the American Revolution, it was a movement not with but against the lead of civilization; and outside of its original limits never struck the spark of sympathy. In 1776, however, the common heart of the whole line of colonies responded to the peril of that one which was first to suffer. In the fall of 1774 met at Philadelphia the original Continental Congress, more with a view to adjustment than to independence. Its professions of loyalty were sincere, and its appeals were not to arms but to the sense of justice in the mother country. But the tide was stronger than those who rode it. The time for the friendly arbitrament of counsel and delay was gone; and when the immortal Second Congress met in Philadelphia, in May, 1775, Patrick Henry had already thundered in the Virginia Convention that there was no peace, that the war had actually begun, and as for him give him liberty or give him death. Lexington green had been crimsoned with the blood of the embattled fathers, and Concord Bridge was already the beginning of our victories, and henceforth the romance of our annals. No congress could make history so fast as it was already making at Bunker Hill, in Gloucester Harbor, along the shores of Quincy and Marshfield, at the entrenchments around Boston, and in the spontaneous outburst of a common enthusiasm, which brought to the camp under Washington, from Carolina, from Virginia, from Pennsylvania, from Maryland, marching over the mountains, and eager for the fray, the sons of sister colonies, the riflemen of Daniel Morgan, the Puritan and cavalier, the woodsmen and farmers, the children of the Huguenots and the Presbyterians.

Carrying out the instruction of his constituents, Richard Henry Lee, of Virginia, the author of the resolution for independence, introduced it into Congress on the 7th of June, 1776. It met with the enthusiastic support of John Adams, who seconded it with a fervor and power that gained him the appellation of the Colossus. It was favored by the subtle and philosophic Franklin, who not only comprehended the grandeur of the occasion, but smarted to repay, in the achieved independence of his country, and in the loss to Great Britain of her brightest jewels, the insults rankling in his breast, which, during his attempt years before to plead the cause of America before the Privy Council in England, had been heaped upon him, amid the sneers of a British ministry, by the stinging tongue of Attorney-General Wedderburne. It was supported, too, by the inflexible will of Sam Adams, and no man had from the earliest more clearly foreseen the result. On the other side was ranged the cautious Dickinson, of Philadelphia, who, till that time the most influential member of Congress, now doubted whether the hour for separation had come, and, doubting, was lost. New York, hesitating to risk its commercial existence, had instructed its delegates, themselves ripe enough for the work, to hold back. South Carolina voted against the resolution. Pennsylvania and Delaware were divided. But these defections were idle. The real resolution of independence had long since been uttered. It had been the staple of every town meeting in America, the subject of every fireside conversation, the thought of every farmer and mechanic; and when the fifty men who assembled in that Congress, adopted by more than a two-thirds vote, in Committee of the Whole, on the first day of July, 1776, the resolution of independence, they but gave expression to the sentiment of America, as also John Adams expressed it in that unpremeditated burst of eloquence, of which no report exists except in the traditions of its magnificent boldness and vigor, and in the imaginary reproduction of Webster. On the second day of July even the fears of the minority were overcome, and the resolution was adopted, without a dissenting vote, that the United Colonies were, and of right ought to be, free and independent States. Two days later, on the Fourth, the day we celebrate, the declaration of principles on which the resolution of independence was founded, drawn by Thomas Jefferson, then thirty-three years of age, and revised by Franklin and Adams, was presented and adopted, and, with the broad sign manual of John Hancock at its foot, became the great charter of the war, the bulletin to England and the world of the justice and dignity of our cause.

Recall the quaint and homely city of Philadelphia; the gloom that hung over it from the terrible responsibility of the step there taken; the modest hall, still standing and baptized as the cradle of liberty. On its tower swung the bell, which yet survives, with its legend, " PROCLAIM LIBERTY THROUGHOUT ALL THE LAND TO ALL THE INHABITANTS THEREOF." That day it rang out a proclamation of liberty that will indeed echo through the land, and in the ears of all the inhabitants thereof, long after the bell itself shall have crumbled into dust. Hancock is in the President's chair; before him sit the half hundred delegates, who at that time represent America.

Among the names it is remarkable how many there are that have since been famous in our annals, — Harrison, Lee, Adams, Clinton, Chase, Stockton, Paine, Hopkins, Wilson, Nelson, Lewis, Walcott, Thompson, Rutledge, and more. The committee appointed to draft the declaration are Jefferson, youngest and tallest; John Adams; Sherman, shoemaker; Franklin, printer; and Robert R. Livingston. If the patriot Sam Adams, at the sunrise of Lexington, could say, "Oh! what a glorious morning for America!" how well might he have renewed, in the more brilliant noontime of July 4, 1776, the same prophetic words! There is nothing in the prophecies of old more striking and impressive than the words of John Adams, who declared the event would be celebrated by succeeding generations as a great anniversary festival, and commemorated as a day of deliverance from one end of the continent to the other; that through all the gloom he could see the light; that the end was worth all the means; and that posterity would triumph in the transaction.

I am not of those who overrate the past. I know that the men of 1776 had the common weaknesses and short-comings of humanity. I read the Declaration of Independence with no feeling of awe; and yet if I were called upon to select from the history of the world any crisis grander, loftier, purer, more heroic, I should know not where to turn. It seems simple enough to-day. There is no schoolboy who will not tell you he knows it by heart; and so much a part of the national fibre is it, that the schoolboy cannot conceive of his or any American's not declaring and doing the same thing. But it was something else that day. The men who signed the Declaration knew not but they were signing warrants for their own

ignominious execution on the gibbet. It was the desperation of the punster's wit that led one of them to say, that
unless they hung together, they would all hang separately.
The bloody victims of the Jacobite rebellions of 1715 and
1745 were still a warning to rebels; and the gory holocaust of Culloden was fresh in the memory. But it was
not only the personal risk; it was risking the homes, the
commerce, the lives, the property, the honor, the future
destiny of three million innocent people, — men, women,
and children. It was defying, on behalf of a straggling
chain of colonies clinging to the seaboard, the most impe-
rial power of the world. It was, more than all, like Co-
lumbus sailing into awful uncertainty of untried space;
casting off from an established and familiar form of government and politics; drifting away to unknown methods,
and upon the dangerous and yawning chaos of democratic
institutions; flying from ills they had to those they knew
not of; and, perhaps, laying the way for a miserable and
bloody catastrophe in anarchy and riot. There are times
when ordinary men are borne by the tide of an occasion
to crests of grandeur in conduct and action. Such a time,
such an occasion, was that which to-day we celebrate.
While the signers of the Declaration were picked men,
none the less true is it that their extraordinary fame is
due not more to their merits than to the crisis at which
they were at the helm, and to the great popular instinct
which they obeyed and expressed.

And so we ask, why do we commemorate with such veneration and display this special epoch and event in our
history; why do we repeat the words our fathers spoke or
wrote; why cherish their names, when our civilization is
better than theirs, and when we have reached in science,
art, education, religion, in politics, in every phase of hu-

man development, even in morals, a higher level? It is because we recognize that in their beginnings the eternal elements of truth and right and justice were conspicuous; and to those eternal verities we pay our tribute, and not to their surroundings, except so far as we poetically let the form stand for the spirit, the man for the idea, the event for the purpose. And it is also because we can do no better work than to perpetuate virtue in the citizen by keeping always fresh in the popular mind, whether we do it by the art of the painter, by oration, or by bonfire, the great heroic deeds and times of our history. In this light it is almost impossible to overrate the influence on national destiny of a legend or a name. Look back to your own childhood and tell me when you first grew mature enough to distinguish patriotism from the story of General Warren and Bunker Hill. Who shall say that the tradition of Marathon and Thermopylæ did not give us Concord and Yorktown, as it also gave independence to modern Greece, and glorified the career and death of Byron, and made our own Howe crusader and philanthropist? Who shall determine how far the maintenance of the integrity of our Union will depend on the memory of Webster, and find help in the picture in Faneuil Hall of his great debate with Hayne, as well as in his unanswerable logic? And who shall say to how great an extent the love of country for the next century shall rise from the fidelity with which we keep alive in the public heart the *memorabilia* of our Revolution and of our recent war? Wise, indeed, as well as loyal and beautiful, is it that to-day all America joins in this observance; that at this hour a thousand orators are speaking words of high emprise; that poets kindle the fire of patriotism, and that the heroes of 1776 stand up from the past, grander and diviner for the illusion of distance, and point the way to the highest ideals of national attainment. The valuable thing in the past is not the man or the event, which are both always ordinary, and which, under the enchantment of distance and the pride of descent, we love to surround with exaggerated glory; it is rather in the sentiment for which the man and the event stand. The ideal is alone substantial and alone survives.

Let us avoid undue praise of the fathers, because the bare truth is tribute enough, and because it is so easy to exaggerate the past. Such undue exaltation of the good of other times has its demoralizing side. There is no service or manliness in belittling our own times and men. We can appreciate the past as well if we appreciate ourselves at our own true value. It is the fashion of the hour — and not a new fashion, especially when partisanship is bitter and searching — to scatter the poison of aspersion on all surrounding character, service, and system. And yet, to my mind, there is occasion for thorough satisfaction with the result of the first century of the republic. It began as an experiment, doubtful and uncertain; it began with nothing more than a feeble union of sentiment, engendered by the enthusiasm of common military service and a common exposure; it began amid a diversity of interests and of races, of religious and ethnic characteristics; it began not only without money, but with a crushing burden of debt which it seemed to have no resources or means of paying; it began with no hold on the cooperation of foreign powers, except the chivalrous sympathy that ended almost with the stirring events of the war that aroused it; it began in a state of public demoralization caused by seven years of campaigning, and with a currency debased and worthless, and furnishing still a terrible warning against the rot which such inflation and depreciation cause in the character, tone, and truth of a people; it began with a discontented and disturbed soldiery, unpaid, destitute, and neglected, and smarting under the ingratitude of their country. Its early years were marked by riots and rebellions. It is claimed that nothing but the firm and enduring weight of the character of Washington held it together. Its constitution was framed and adopted only with reluctance and doubt. The morals of the people were not of a high order. The morals of public men were low. Aaron Burr was of a character so notoriously infamous, that to-day it is incredible how he could have been chosen Vice-President and brought within two or three votes of the Presidency itself. Hamilton was not free from reproach. Religion, when not asleep, was coarse and illiterate. Congress was the scene of debates bitter and personal to a shameful degree. The Cabinet was divided against itself. The mutual hate of Jefferson and Hamilton it would be hard to parallel. Vituperation, abuse, and slander poisoned many an honest name; and though now, the mist of prejudice having lifted, we look back and see only what was solid and valuable growth, yet in that day it was said, as we hear it said nowadays, that corruption was undermining the foundations, and that democracy was a demonstrated failure.

Read the journal of John Quincy Adams, and note what half a century ago was his estimate of the selfishness, meanness, vulgarity, and hopelessness of the public service; how speedily he looked for the disruption of a brittle republic, and with what contempt he refers to Webster and Clay, and the names we have been taught to reverence. We must not be blinded by the miasma of present abuse which is always afloat. We must take deeper views and a wider range. Look not at any year, but on the whole century, and see what has been the advance, what the progress in arts, in science, in human life and culture, in all that broadens the intellect and enlarges the soul, in all that humanizes and educates a people! The feeble colonies are an empire so magnificent in territory and population that the imagination cannot take it in. The imperfect league of 1776 is the majestic consolidated nation of thirty-eight States, each one an empire, and the whole the most magnificent and forward cluster of civil polity the world ever saw, — a very well-spring of human enlightenment and outgrowth in every upward direction. The national government, which was almost overthrown, even under the guard of Washington, by a whiskey riot in a ravine of the Alleghanies, has withstood the shock of a civil war which rocked a continent to its foundations, triumphing not so much by force of arms as by the popular sense of right, and rising from the convulsion stronger than ever, by reason of the eradication of the one false and diseased element which impaired it and which was, from the first, an element of weakness as it was of wrong. Think of what has been done in the matter of education, of public schools, of universities of learning for both sexes and all races. In science we have unlocked the secrets of the earth and the air and the sea, and made them not merely matters of wonder, but handmaidens of homely use. Religion has been refined and elevated, and the human mind, searching for divine truth, has risen above superstition and cant, and, with knowledge for its guide, has reconciled faith with an enlightened reason. In all matters of comfort, of use, of elegance, of convenient living, of house, and table, and furniture, and light, and warmth, and health, and travel, what thorough and beneficent advance equally for all, shaming the petty meanness with which, unjust alike to the old times and the new, we inveigh against the new times and overrate the old! At home it is with a feeling of satisfaction and pride that we turn to our own Commonwealth in every department of her public life; in her spotless judiciary, which has never fallen below its best standard, and whose ermine bears no stain; or her legislature, which has always expressed the popular will, and embodied in its enactments the reach of the popular sentiment. Shall I prefer the old times, when I see government made to-day the use, the culture, the salvation of the people; saving those who are in peril from want and fire and famine; looking after the little children; caring for the insane, the idiotic, the criminal, the drunkard, the unfortunate, the orphans, and the aged; guarding the interests of the laborer; bringing to the help of the agriculturist the best results of science, and building colleges for the promotion of the noble calling of the culture of the soil; guarding the savings of the small earners; investigating the causes of disease, and securing its prevention; giving to all the people comforts that were once not even the luxurious dreams of princes; pouring out education like streams of living water; maintaining great and generous charities, and extending the shield of its foresight and encouragement over all alike? Grant that since the rebellion of 1861, as years ago after the revolution of 1776, a period of war was followed by an extraordinary period of demoralization, resulting from the excessive and abnormal disturbance of the ordinary channels of labor and industry, and especially from that inflation of our currency which gave rise to incredible increase of expenditure and debt, and from which recovery came only with a shock. Grant that corruption sometimes exists in high places and in low; grant that politics are too often turned into barter. Whatever the evil, it cannot stand against the discernment which is so swift to uncover and shame it, and which will permit it no concealment. And there is good token in the very sensitiveness of the public mind, which was never keener or quicker to discover and punish fraud and faithlessness than now. It must not be forgotten that the republic not only was an experiment in its inception, but is so still. We are apt to judge by the severe rules of criticism which we apply to completed work. We forget that only a few short years ago it was said that a popular government cannot succeed; that the popular mind is not sufficiently educated to be relied on; that a pure democracy has in it no stability or permanence, but must go down with the first tumult of popular frenzy; that patriotism will decay without the veneration that attaches to monarchy; and that in a government of the people, ignorance, fraud, brutality, and crime will rise, by might of fist and lung, to the supremacy. The wonder is, not that the republic is not perfect to-day in its machinery, its character, its results, but that, with its monstrous expansion from within and immigration from abroad, it has fared so well, and that its achievements are better than its founders dared predict or hope. Tell me what government, ancient or modern, has been more stable, or freer from convulsion. Who are our politicians, if not our presidents of colleges, our brightest poets, our most vigorous divines, our conspicuous merchants, our foremost lawyers, our leading men everywhere? Our politics, at which we rail so much, are what we are. Will you say that there are startling evidences of neglect, when no pulpit is without its fervid appeal for loftier patriotism; when no class graduates from college that half its orations are not on the duty of the citizen to the state; when our centennials fairly weary us with the demand, made by all who speak by voice or pen, for national purity and virtue; and when no political party dares the popular verdict that does not proclaim and exhibit its purpose of reform in every branch of the public service? Let the test of our hope or despair be not so much the severe standard of the very highest reach of the demands of to-day, but rather the modest trust with which a hundred years ago our fathers risked a democracy. Is it nothing that their perilous confidence in human nature, and in the ability and inclination of the masses to govern themselves aright, has been justified and not abused? Is it nothing that, ruled by a mob, our leaders selected from and by a mob, our laws the popular sentiment of a mob, yet such is the preponderance of the good elements over the bad, of the upward tendency over the downward, of order over disorder, of progress over stagnation, that the experiment has resulted in a century of success; that, however imperfect the scheme in some of its outward manifestations, it is correct in principle; and that it has demonstrated the practicability and wisdom of a government of the people, by the people, for the people? If there were none in the ranks except the men who have proved unworthy, we might despair; but not when we remember that in every section of the country we still number great hosts of honest and able men fit for every political need or duty. If a period of national demoralization were followed by continued indifference and acquiescence, we might despair; but not when we see it followed by the indignant uprising of the better elements, the wholesome criticism of the press, the outcry of the poet and the philosopher, the sturdy and resolute reaction of that fundamental intelli-

gence and honesty of the people, which are the fruit of
our system of free education, and which can always be relied on in the last resort to do the work of reform when
the crisis comes. For one I feel no anxiety. I regard it
as a sign of the permanence of our institutions, that to-
day, when so many mourn over the sadder revelations of
the time, a wiser philosophy looks through the ferment
that is sloughing the scum from the surface and purifying
the body politic from top to bottom. To be conscious of
the malady, in a republic of free schools and a free press,
is to cure it.

It is easy to raise spectres of danger, and forecast perils that threaten to destroy the republic. But it will meet
and beat them. It is flying in the face of nature and of
experience to fear that man, with increasing expansion
of his opportunities and powers, has, like a child, no horizon of promise beyond his present vision. Why should
we at the approach of the next century, with its magnificent impulse onward, shudder with the same ignorant
and ungodly distrust with which the old time trembled
at the coming of our own ? We have brought no dangers
that we have not averted, no perils that have overwhelmed
us. Why whisper under the breath that in the near years
to come men are to withdraw more and more from the
grinding of unremitted and unlightened physical toil ?
Do not you and I enjoy whatever exemption from it there
comes to us ; and shall not the humblest enjoy as much ?
Will it be an evil when science, with its inventions and
its use of the illimitable agencies of nature, the development of which is now but in its infancy, performs still
more the drudgery of toil and lets the souls of all go
freer ? Labor and industry, in the nature of things, will
never cease ; but the progress of the ages will direct them

to higher levels of employment, never dispensing with
their need, but rather adding to their dignity and to the
happiness they return. Why, too, this terror lest those,
who have not had the sweetness and refinements and elevation of leisure, shall have them more and more, as well
as those to whom it certainly has brought, not harm, but
culture ? Has the result hitherto been so disastrous as to
make us fear either the bettered conditions of the masses,
or their ambition for better conditions still ? Faith in
the common people is not a fine phrase or a dream ; it is
the teaching of experience and test. They, too, may be
confided in to measure and accept the necessities and inequalities that attach to human living ; and they are not
going to destroy any social econo. y which blesses them
all, because it does not bless them all alike. Are not
fidelity, patience, loyal service, and good citizenship, true
of the kitchen, the loom, and the bench ? Is there no
professor's chair, no clergyman's desk, no merchant
prince's counting-room, dishonored ? Does, indeed, the
line of simple worth or social or political stability run on
the border of any class or station ? The people may be
trusted with their own interests. If it shall appear that
any one form of government or society fails, there will
always be intelligence and wit enough to fashion a better.
Forces will come at command. The instinct of self-pre-
servation counts for something, as well as the elements
of goodness and progress which are inherent in human
nature. And when all these unite, while there will indeed be change and revolution, there will never be wreck
and chaos. There will be fools and fanatics and assas-
sins and demagogues and nihilists, and all sorts of insane or vicious dissolvers of security ; there will be con-
vulsions and horrors : every fair summer the lightning

flashes and strikes. But all these are the tempests of the year against the unfailing sunshine and rain which make the blooming and fragrant garden of the earth. There must, indeed, be eternal vigilance and increasing zeal and endeavor for the right. But can there be nobler or finer service than to contribute these? Or, if you, sleek and well-to-do and jealous of your fortunate share of good things, fear lest frenzy and drunkenness and vice invade your domain, will you not stop sneering at the reformers, who, in whatever line or of whatever sex or social scale, are trying to breast the torrent, and give them your countenance, your help, and your right arm? Shall our forecast of imminent or coming perils unnerve us and awake only a whine of despair; or shall it rather put us to our mettle, and to the development of the better influences which always have averted and always will avert disaster?

Grant the great accumulations of individual and corporate wealth, with its larger luxuries; grant this, and, if there be danger in it, — as there is, — be on your guard. But is it all evil? Have the multitude been correspondingly straitened and deprived? Are the homes, the food, the clothing, the literary and æsthetic tastes, and the amusements of the toilers, more limited, or do they share in the general betterment? Is the public library closed to them? Is there no newspaper — a library in itself — in their hands each day? Have they less or dimmer light to read by than before; or scantier means of conveyance from the city to the fields and beach; or more meagre communication with the great orbit of the living world, its interests, its activities, its resources? May we not yet find even in this bugbear of excessive wealth, with its perilous luxury emasculating those who enjoy it and tempting those who ape it, the seeds of the evil's own cure? If it be not so, it is the first instance of a corruption which has not wrought its own better life. Need we, indeed even now, look far off for a day when the vulgar gluttony of wealth will be the disdain of good manners and high character, not worth its own heavy weight, and no longer the aim of a better and finer time? Is happiness, or was it ever, correspondent with wealth or luxury? Are not most men superior to either, or to the fever for them? I do not think it too much to say, that in the time to come, " Give me neither poverty nor riches " will be not only the wise man's prayer, but the " smart " man's maxim and the aristocrat's choice. What refreshment, even to-day, to turn to examples of wealth, — of which so many are illustrious in your own city, — which finds its most gracious use and its most indulgent luxury in cooling streams of charity and beneficence flowing broadcast amid the parched lowlands of want and ignorance and wrong! Under our system the easy mobility of wealth is its own no small safeguard and regulator. Not only do fortunes come and go ; not only from all rounds of the social ladder do the millionaires spring ; but, even while retained in the same hand, wealth does not lie inactive and embayed, but is coursing everywhere, a trust rather than an exclusive possession to its owner, employing, supporting, enriching, a thousand other men. To assail it is to attack not him, but them. It is engaged in their service more than in his. It has no existence except in this very subservience to the general use. Destroy this function, and it is but a corpse, worth no man's having. Fortunate is the community, and men do not decay, where, under our institutions, wealth accumulates. It cannot fill one hand without

overflowing into every other. It cannot live to itself
alone.

Danger and peril enough indeed; need everywhere for
safeguards and forethought! But the world is a failure
and man is a lie if there be not in him the capacity to
rise to his own might, and to keep pace with his own
growth. Are education, science, is this godlike mind,
are the soul and the moral nature, to count for nothing
but their own disaster? Is there no future manhood to
meet the future crisis? Is there no God? As the dead
past buries its dead, so the unborn future will solve its own
needs. Ours it is to do the duty of the present hour.

And to that high duty with what a trumpet-call are we
summoned! I would at once avoid indiscriminate praise
or blame of the things of to-day. I would not so assail
our national and social and political character and men
and institutions as to destroy our self-respect; nor, on
the other hand, would I shut my eyes to the glaring de-
fects that exist, and that are a reproach to any people.
There is rust upon our escutcheon. Our civil service
cries aloud for the reform which has begun to come, and
which is already shaping the action of politicians and
departments that are unconsciously obeying the public
sentiment it has created. There is sometimes lack of
homely honesty in our touch upon the public money;
there is dishonor in high places; there are frauds in
finance. But these are evils not permanent in the heart
of a progressive people. They are only incidental to in-
complete systems. They suggest what would be a nobler
and more vital theme for us at this time than even the
Declaration of Independence of 1776; and that is a new
and present declaration of independence, which, if pro-
claimed to the world in honesty and sincerity, would

make some John Adams of to-day prophesy that it would be henceforward celebrated by succeeding generations from one end of the continent to the other.

The century just past was a century of military and political growth; the century opening this hour will be one of moral and scientific growth. The parties of the future can only succeed if they embody some great moral element and purpose. Let us have here and now a new declaration of independence, — independence from ignorance and prejudice and narrowness and false restraint; from the ruthless machinery of war, so that we may have the beneficent influences of peace; from the clumsiness of any lingering barbarism, so that we may have the full development of a Christian civilization; from the crimes that infest and retard society; from intemperance and drunkenness and false gods; from low views of public trust. No declaration of the fathers would compare for a moment with a declaration of the high moral purposes that beckon us on to a loftier national life. The field is unlimited; the opportunity for growth inexhaustible. Only let us realize the absolute duty of impressing on the leading classes, as we call them, on the educated and religious classes, at least, the necessity of their projecting themselves out of the ranks which need no physician into the ranks which do. I do not mean the nonsense of class distinctions; I mean that whoever is a foremost man in any sphere, in the professions, in trade or elsewhere, whoever leads in politics, in church, in society, in the shop, must feel that on his shoulders alone rests the public safety.

There must be the sense of personal obligation on every man whose natural power or happy opportunities have given him a lift in any wise above the rest. Virtue, pub-

lic and private, will become easy and popular when it is
the badge and inspiration of the leaders ; and good influences from the top will permeate through the whole
body politic as rain filters through the earth and freshens
it with verdure and beauty and fertility. I would em-
phasize, more than anything else, the duty of the enlightened classes to throw all their energies into the popular arena. Why should the ingenuous youth, fresh from
college, dream of Pericles swaying with consummate address and eloquence the petty democracy of Athens, and
himself shun the town house where, in a golden age beside which the age of Pericles is brass, is moulded the
destiny of his own magnificent republic ? Why kindle
with the invective of Cicero, or the wit of Aristophanes,
and himself be too dainty to lift voice or finger to banish
Catiline and Cleon from manipulating the honor, the
integrity, the achievement, of the fatherland, bequeathed
to him in sacred trust by his own heroic ancestors?
Little sympathy is to be felt with the spirit that stands
aloof and rails at the clumsy work of a government by
the people, who, on their part, invariably welcome the
approach of the man of culture, and will give him place
if only he will not convey the idea that he despises it.
It is useless to deny that the scholars have failed oftentimes — less of late — to improve their opportunity ; and
if ever the republic goes to the bad, it will be, not because the illiterate and lax have seized and depraved it,
but because the instructed and trained have neglected it.

To me it seems axiomatic that the educated and virtu-
ous, in a free state, can control it if they will. Here we
are at the threshold of these great economic questions of
labor, of capital, of currency. They affect the very
tables and hearthstones and muscles of us all. We have

yet to solve the problem of so distributing the excess of the grain of the world that no man shall be unable to fairly exchange his product for it; of so distributing the excess of wealth that no man shall be destitute who is willing to work. There will be fewer frauds upon the revenue as commerce is gradually relieved from its restraints. Defalcations will be rare when the proper channels for capital are alone open and the eddies and cataracts of baseless speculation are avoided. There will be no terrorism of strikes when labor is directed aright and its wages are its honest measure. There will be no bubbles to burst, no corners for the gamblers to work up, when the laws that regulate the carrying of the product to the consumer are learned, and the supply becomes a steady stream, flowing into and satisfying the demand. All these are the questions of the economy of the future. There lies before us a field which should make the heart of a true man glad as he sees approaching a century of peace, of wise economies, of amelioration for the masses, of opportunity for lifting all men to a happy and useful activity. So shall those who follow reap a grander harvest than ours. It is God's earth, and He made it for His children. How the arts will educate and train them; how science will enlighten them; how great moral strides will take them to loftier planes of conduct and life! There can be no failure of the republic among an intelligent people, with schools for the young, with good examples in the past, with Christian ideals for the future. It has already surmounted its most stupendous risks and assaults. It has ridden them all safely over. The late civil war will only cement the structure. I am told that on the battlefields of Virginia, so swift is time's erasure, where, now seventeen years ago, the land was rough with the intrenchments of the camp, already new woody growths have covered them over, and the foliage and the turf and the fruitful farms bear no mark of war, but wave with lines of beauty and of harvest. So be it, too, in the nation at large! The contest is over; the wrong is righted; the curse is off; the land is redeemed; the sweet angels of peace and reconciliation are flitting from door to door, sitting at the tents, inspiring kinder thoughts and sympathies, and awakening at this very hour the ancient memories of a common sacrifice and a common glory. The great prolific fields of the South, its rivers and natural resources, saved from the blight of slavery, will be the loom and granary and wealth of us all. The softening influences of a common interest will draw together the people of all sections. Commerce and trade and learning, and all the affiliations that interweave the affections of a people, will surround and sustain the central pillar of a common country and destiny.

I am now the hundreth in that succession with whom Boston has charged her Fourth of July orations. Our beloved country is more than a hundred years old. A century has come and has gone. It is indeed but as a day; yet what a day! Not the short and sullen day of the winter solstice, but the long, glorious, and prolific summer day of June. It rose in the twilight glimmerings of the dawn of Lexington, and its rays, falling on the mingled dew and gore of that greensward, and a little later across the rebel gun-barrels of Bunker Hill, and then tenderly lingering on the dead, upturned face of Warren, broke in the full splendor of the first Fourth of July, and lay warm upon the bell in the tower of Independence Hall, as it rang out upon the air the cry of a free nation newly born. Its morning sun, now radiant and now obscured, shone over the battlefields of the Revolution, over the ice of the Delaware, and over the ramparts at York-town swept by the onslaught of the chivalrous Lafayette. It looked down upon the calm figure of Washington in-augurating the new government under the Constitution. It saw the slow but steady consolidation of the Union. It saw the marvelous stride with which, in the early years of the present century, the republic grew in wealth and population, sending its ships into every sea, and its pio-neers into the wilds of the Oregon and to the lakes of the North. It burst through the clouds of the War of 1812, and saw the navy of the young nation triumph in en-counters as romantic as those of armed knights in tour-nament. It heard the arguments of Madison, Hamil-ton, Marshal, Story, and Webster, determining the scope of the Constitution, and establishing forever the theory of its powers and restrictions. It beheld the overthrow of the delusion which regarded the United States as a league and not a nation, and that would have sapped it with the poison of nullification and secession. It saw an era of literature begin, distinguished by the stately achievements of the historian, the thought of the philosopher, the grace of oratory, the sweet pure verse of the American poets, — poets of nature and the heart. It brought the tender ministry of unconsciousness to human pain. It caught the song of machinery, the thunder of the locomotive, the first click of the telegraph. It saw the measureless West unfold its prairies into great activities of life and product and wealth. It saw the virtue and culture and thrift of New England flow broad across the Mississippi, over the Rocky Mountains, and down the Pacific slope, expanding into a civilization so magnificent that its power and grandeur and influence to-day overshadow indeed the fount from which they sprang. It saw America, first wrenching liberty for itself from the hand of European tyranny, share it free as the air with the oppressed and cramped peoples of Europe, carrying food to them in their starvation, offering them an asylum, welcoming their coöperation in the development and enjoyment of the generous culture and freedom and opportunity of the New World, and setting them, from the first even till now, an example of free institutions and local popular government, which every intelligent and self-respecting people must follow. Its afternoon was indeed overcast with shameful assault made on an unoffending neighbor to strengthen the hold of slavery upon the misguided interests of the country; and there came the fiery tempest of civil war: the heart of the nation mourned the slaughter of its patriots, and the treason and folly of its children of the South, yet welcomed them back to their place in the family circle. And now eventide has come; the storm is over; the long day has drawn to its close in the magnificent irradiation that betokens a glorious morning. We gather at our thresholds and hold sweet neighborly converse. Our children are about us in pleasant homes; our flocks are safe; our fields are ripening with the harvest. We recall the day, and pray that the God of the pilgrim and the patriot will make the morrow of our republic even brighter and better. May it indeed be the land of the free, — the land of education and virtue, in which there shall be none ignorant or depraved, none outside the pale of the influence and sympathy of the best, and therefore no swift or slow declension to corruption and death, no decline or fall for the future historian to write.